BRIGHT NOTES

THE LEAVES OF GRASS BY WALT WHITMAN

Intelligent Education

Nashville, Tennessee

BRIGHT NOTES: The Leaves of Grass
www.BrightNotes.com

No part of this publication may be used or reproduced in any manner whatsoever without written permission, except in the case of brief quotations in critical articles and reviews. For permissions, contact Influence Publishers http://www.influencepublishers.com.

ISBN: 978-1-645425-32-8 (Paperback)
ISBN: 978-1-645425-33-5 (eBook)

Published in accordance with the U.S. Copyright Office Orphan Works and Mass Digitization report of the register of copyrights, June 2015

Originally published by Monarch Press.
Randall Hughes Keenan, 1965
2020 Edition published by Influence Publishers.

Interior design by Lapiz Digital Services. Cover Design by Thinkpen Designs.

Printed in the United States of America.

Library of Congress Cataloging-in-Publication Data forthcoming.
Names: Intelligent Education
Title: BRIGHT NOTES: The Leaves of Grass
Subject: STU004000 STUDY AIDS / Book Notes

CONTENTS

1) Introduction to Walt Whitman — 1

2) Inscriptions — 9

3) Starting From Paumanok — 17

4) Textual Analysis — 28
   - Sections 1-16 — 28
   - Sections 17-38 — 47
   - Sections 39-52 — 68

5) Children of Adam — 83

6) Two Final Poems — 100

7) Calamus — 103

8) Drum-Taps — 118

9) Out of the Cradle Endlessly Rocking — 141

10) When Lilacs Last In The Dooryard Bloom'd — 152

11)	Crossing Brooklyn Ferry	168
12)	Walt Whitman Today	178
13)	Questions and Answers For Review	181
14)	Topics For Research Reports	189
15)	Annotated Bibliographical Guide	191

INTRODUCTION TO WALT WHITMAN

I assume that Poetry in America needs to be entirely recreated ... literature which will be our own; with neither foreign spirit, nor imagery nor form, but adapted to our case, grown out of our associations, boldly portraying the West, strengthening and intensifying the national soul, and finding the entire fountains of its birth and growth in our own country.

Letter from Walt Whitman to William D. O'Connor, 1866.

WHITMAN'S EARLY YEARS: 1819-1849

In *Leaves of Grass*, Walt Whitman wrote:

> Take my leaves America, take them South,
>   and take them North,
> Make welcome for them everywhere,
>   for they are your own offspring, ...
>
> "Starting from Paumanok"

Eventually, America did take Whitman's "leaves" and honored them as a great contribution to the literature of our country. The

"Good Gray Poet," as his friend and defender, William O'Connor, called him in 1866, is praised by many critics today as our greatest native American poet. However, great poets often have humble beginnings; and Walt Whitman was no exception. He was born on May 31, 1819, the son of Walter and Louisa Van Velsor Whitman, on an unprosperous farm at West Hills, Long Island. His family came from Welsh-Quaker, Dutch, and English stock; and in his own words he was "Well begotten, and rais'd by a perfect mother." In 1923 the family moved to Brooklyn, New York. By 1830, at the age of eleven, young Whitman's formal schooling came to an end. He was put to work running errands and doing chores, at first in a doctor's office and soon afterward for a lawyer. Whitman was an enthusiastic reader, and it may have been in these surroundings that he began his lifelong love for the works of the nineteenth century English novelist, Sir Walter Scott.

Whitman then became a printer's helper and soon afterward began to do some newspaper work. In the late 1830s, he returned to Long Island, or, as he liked to refer to it by its Indian name, Paumanok. He traveled about from town to town as a schoolteacher and soon edited his own newspaper, the Long Islander, at Huntington. By 1841 Whitman could be considered a professional journalist and writer. He did editorial work, wrote verse, and contributed to newspapers in the New York area. In 1846, at the age of 27, he became the editor of the *Brooklyn Daily Eagle*, a liberal Democratic newspaper. After two years, Whitman journeyed south and edited the recently founded *New Orleans Crescent*. However, it was only two months later that Whitman, his spirit searching and unsettled, left New Orleans to travel along the Mississippi River, to move on to Chicago and the Great Lakes region, and to see Niagara Falls. By the fall of 1848, he was back in Brooklyn editing the Freeman, a newspaper connected with the Free-Soil party. Whitman was opposed to slavery;

and the Free-Soil party, with its fight to prevent the extension of that evil into areas of our country that had not yet become states, appealed to the young poet. It was scarcely a year later, however, that Whitman was prompted to resign his position on the Freeman as a result of political differences. These were restless years for him and he was in search of positive direction and meaning for his life - and a way of expressing it. The trivial rivalries of party politics had proven far too narrow for the man and poet who would soon write: "I hear America singing, the varied carols I hear."

THE GREAT POET: 1850-1873

While building houses and working as a carpenter in Brooklyn between 1850 and 1854, Whitman composed some of the poems that would appear in the collection of verse, *Leaves of Grass*. In early July of 1855, the book was published; and by 1860 two more editions were issued. During these years, with his literary position still uncertain, Whitman wrote for Life Illustrated and once again took up his work in journalism, this time as an editor of the Brooklyn Times. By 1860 the poet could be found amid the sordid atmosphere of Pfaff's, a famous Bohemian restaurant and meeting place for artists and writers in nineteenth century New York.

On April 12, 1860, the South fired upon Fort Sumter; the Civil War had begun. In 1862 the poet's brother George was wounded. Whitman traveled to Virginia to be near him and to act as a type of volunteer army nurse. During the war years, Whitman visited wounded soldiers in the hospitals, suffered from poor health himself, and worked for various government offices in Washington. It was the Civil War and the assassination of President Abraham Lincoln on April 14, 1865 that deeply affected the poet and inspired some of his finest poetry - the collection *Drum-Taps* and the splendid tribute to Lincoln, "When Lilacs Last in the Dooryard Bloom'd."

In 1865 Whitman was forced to leave his position in a government office. A superior who believed, as many people did, that *Leaves of Grass* was an immoral book, discovered that he was its author and discharged him. However, Whitman was reinstated in government employment and remained with the Civil Service until 1873.

Whitman's reputation flourished abroad, and he even received a marriage proposal from an English widow, Mrs. Anne Gilcrist. She was an intelligent but emotional woman who had completed her late husband Alexander Gilcrist's, biography of the English poet William Blake and had fallen in love with Whitman after reading his *Children of Adam* poems. She confessed to possessing a "loving ardent aspiring soul," and even visited the 53-year-old poet in America in 1876. Discreetly, Whitman declined her offer, and she returned to England.

The early 1870s witnessed some recognition of Whitman as poet. He appeared at the Dartmouth College commencement in 1872, where he delivered "As a Strong Bird on Pinions Free," later to be called "Thou Strong Mother with Thy Equal Brood." In this poem he reaffirmed his faith in America, the "Brain of the New World," and honored it as the "ship of Democracy."

YEARS OF DECLINE: 1873-1892

In January of 1873, Whitman suffered a paralytic stroke. He had passed the "high plateau" of his life, and the peak of his creative power was behind him. The later years saw his poem "Song of the Universal" read at the Tufts College commencement in Massachusetts; the heated public controversy over his literary neglect by America; Boston's effort to "clean up" the 1881 edition of *Leaves of Grass*; his meeting with the English poet and playwright, Oscar Wilde; the publication of notebook jottings and diary entries, *Specimen Days and Collect*, in 1883; a Whitman biography by Richard Bucke in the same year; and retirement to Camden, New Jersey, in 1884. At Camden a "Whitman Fellowship" formed around him, and he received some of that intimate veneration from admirers that few great poets are able to enjoy during their lifetimes.

When Whitman died on March 26, 1892, he was an American poet whose artistic vision was perhaps too broad and penetrating for his times. His genius and art were too rare and distinct for the **conventions** of his day. A good appraisal of the poet might be that of the nineteenth century English author and critic, John Addington Symonds, who wrote of Whitman in 1893: "Speaking about him is like speaking about the universe."

GROWTH OF THE POET AND THE BOOK

Leaves of Grass was not a collection of poetry to be published and set aside by its author. The book grew and expanded almost in the same way as the "Grass" of its title. It was not intended by Whitman to be dead poetry, but verses that were alive, reflective of the vitality of the common man and of the electric excitement that Whitman perceived in the democracy of America and in her future. He had extraordinary poetic vision; he could see the whole spectrum of American life - collective, individual, and personal: "The United States with veins full of poetical stuff."

In early July of 1855, *Leaves of Grass* was published; it eventually appeared in nine editions during the poet's lifetime. Ironically, when the book was circulated, Whitman did not achieve his intended purpose. The poems were aimed at the average everyday man, since Whitman had no respect for old aristocratic notions. His "aristocracy" was populated by the glorified common man in the richness of American democracy - a man like "Walt Whitman, an American, one of the roughs." However, it was not the common man who gave his approval to *Leaves of Grass*, but intellectuals such as the famous American philosopher and poet, Ralph Waldo Emerson. Only a few days after *Leaves of Grass* came into print, Emerson wrote to Whitman from Concord, Massachusetts:

> **I am not blind to the wonderful gift of *Leaves of Grass*. I find it the most extraordinary piece of wit & wisdom that America has yet contributed . . . I have great joy in it. I find incomparable things said incomparably well, as they must be . . . I greet you at beginning of a great career, . . . I rubbed my eyes to see if this sunbeam were no illusion; but the solid sense of the book is a sober certainty.**

When the great seventeenth century English poet John Milton wrote that "A good book is the precious life-blood of a master-spirit,: he might well have been looking two hundred odd years ahead to Walt Whitman and *Leaves of Grass*. Whitman's poetry was a great outflowing of himself and his ideals. Of the twelve untitled poems that represented the first edition, the best was a long and deeply personal work. It occupied about half of the book's total length, and was not permanently entitled "Song of Myself" until 1881. In 1856 Whitman issued a second edition of *Leaves of Grass*, which was now expanded to well over three hundred and fifty pages. He assigned titles to each poem and added twenty new ones, including what is now the famous "Crossing Brooklyn Ferry." In 1860, the four-hundred-and-fifty-page third edition of *Leaves of Grass* experienced even greater reshaping than did the edition of 1856. Whitman added one hundred and twenty-four new poems, experimented with new titles for many of the older ones, and revised many of the poems from previous editions. This was a period of enormous creativity for him. It produced "A Word out of the Sea," later to be entitled "Out of the Cradle Endlessly Rocking" - a poem which must be placed among his best and most beautiful. In a letter to his brother Jeff in May of 1860, Whitman remarked that he was

. . . very, very much satisfied and relieved that the thing [*Leaves of Grass*], in the permanent form it now is, looks as well and reads as well (to my own notion) as I anticipated - because a good deal, after all, was an experiment - and now I am satisfied.

In 1865, Whitman published his Civil War and Lincoln poems - *Drum-Taps* in June of that year and *Sequel to Drum-Taps* in the autumn. This latter group contained a poem that must certainly be placed among his masterpieces. "When Lilacs Last in the Dooryard Bloom'd" with its somber beauty and measured poetic movement. These two groups of poems were added to the 1868 edition of *Leaves of Grass*, unifying the results of his extremely creative was period. The great change in the fourth edition was the arrangement of the poems. Even though he had never been a soldier, Whitman translated the war's emotion and intensity into poetry of experience that brought fresh life rushing through the new edition and made extensive rearrangement necessary. The poet was not ignorant of the fact that the war period had impelled him to a new creative capacity. In 1863 he wrote to his friend, Charles Eldridge:

> If feel to devote myself more to the work of my life, which is making poems, I must bring out Drum Taps. I must be continually bringing out poems - now is the hey day. I shall range along the high plateau of my life & capacity for a few years now, & then swiftly descend.

In 1871 Whitman published the fifth edition of *Leaves of Grass*, and in 1876 he issued a Centennial Edition which appeared in two volumes. The edition of Whitman's poems which contained the final arrangement was that of 1881-2. The publication of the book had to be transferred from Boston to Philadelphia in 1882, when Boston officials threatened to prosecute unless what they considered to be objectionable passages were eliminated. In a letter to his friend and defender, William O'Connor, on May 25, 1882, Whitman could see beyond the growing pains of *Leaves of Grass* and comment prophetically upon the future of his poetry:

> . . . as to this last & in some sense most marked buffeting in the fortunes of *Leaves of Grass* . . . I shall . . . tickle myself with the thought how it may be said years hence that at any rate no book on earth ever had such a history -

INSCRIPTIONS

BACKGROUND

When Whitman made the final arrangement of *Leaves of Grass*, he place a group of twenty-four poems, titled *Inscriptions*, at the beginning. These short poems were first published between 1860 and 1881, and were included in the various editions of *Leaves of Grass* as they appeared. The *Inscriptions* are intended to identify the themes, directions, and range of ideas that the poet explores in the large single poems and groups of poems that follow.

THEMES

Whitman begins his *Inscriptions* with "One's-Self I Sing." At the very beginning, the poem states a **theme** that lies at the heart of *Leaves of Grass*: the search to identify "self," the individual as a single person and in relation to the whole society of other individuals:

> **One's-Self I sing, a simple separate person,**
> **Yet utter the word Democratic, the word En-Masse.**

Man is precious and significant, individually and together with other men in a democratic society; this is what Whitman will celebrate. The poet is not concerned simply with the idea of mass man, collected an unrefined. He dearly loves democracy and sees it as the best social medium for the perfection of America and her people.

Originally, these short poems were scattered throughout other sections of Leaves; but Whitman collected them and placed them at the head of his poetry. They do not contain broadly developed themes,. but are more like sketches of what is to come. Whitman intends to exclude nothing; no subject can be objectionable if it relates to man and his existence. Poetically, he is a free spirit able to write of

> . . . life and death, for the Body and for the eternal Soul,
> "As I Ponder'd in Silence"
>
> Of Physiology from top to toe I sing,
> . . . . .
>
> The Female equally with the Male I sing.
> One's-Self I Sing"

The great forces of life and society will fill his poetry:

> O Life immense in passion, pulse, and power, . . .
> "One's-Self I Sing".
>
> America's busy, teeming, intricate whirl, . . .
> "Eidolons"
>
> And to define America, her athletic Democracy, . . .

"To Foreign Lands"

| **WHITMAN'S PERSONA**

In "Me Imperturbe," meaning literally, "Me - calm and unmoved," Whitman begins in a boastful and robust manner:

> Me imperturbe, standing at ease in Nature,
> Master of all or mistress of all, aplomb in the midst of irrational
> things,
> Imbued as they, passive, receptive, silent as they,
>
> . . . . .
>
> Me toward the Mexican sea, or in the Mannahatta or the Tennessee,
> or the far north or inland,
> A river man, or a man of the woods or of any farm-life of these States
> or of the coast, or the lakes of Kanada,
> Me wherever my life is lived, . . .

In these lines Whitman begins to "divide" his personality between the figure of Walt Whitman, a single identifiable man, and that of a spirit representative of the American people and their land. His relationship with nature is intimate and compatible; he is nature's own child, going where life leads him. However, Whitman adds a broader, hazier, more universal character to his poetic voice. This mask, or other "personality" through which Whitman speaks, is known in literature as a persona, and is woven in as a very important part of *Leaves of Grass*. By assuming a persona, a poet can act in exceptional ways and say many extraordinary things that would be impossible to say if the poetic voice were to represent only that of a single ordinary man, the poet himself. With the freedom that his persona allows, Whitman can appear as himself - Walt Whitman, poet - and also be detached as the spirit of all individuals, all common Americans. He can be the voice of nature in all its beauties, the champion of American democracy, and the spokesman of all Americans in the diversity of their occupations. Whitman speaks as the champion of American Everyman; his persona and the freedom it provides allow him to be a part of that very thing he observes. When we realize that Whitman uses a persona in *Leaves of Grass*, we can understand how the poet is able to speak, sometimes autobiographically in his own voice, sometimes, affectionately, often boastfully or as a more universal representative, mystically on other occasions, or as a union of voices.

WHITMAN AND AMERICA

Whitman seems to face in all directions at the same time:

> We pass through Kanada, the North-east, the vast valley
> of the Mississippi, and the Southern States, . . .
>
> "On Journeys Through the States"

The scope that Whitman is to cover in *Leaves of Grass* is a vast one. His poetic gaze takes in all of America, the spirit of her citizens, and their democratic society. In "I Hear America Singing," the voices of the people come alive; Whitman demonstrates the great power of his lyrical love of America and his glorification of the common man. In Whitman's poetry, the common man is a very special individual whose Americanism makes him very "uncommon." His special attraction and merit arise from the fact that he is part of the American spirit of democracy and hope, of an America whose bright future is always bound up with Whitman's poetic vision. For Walt Whitman, America is extraordinary because of the union and force of unextraordinary everyday people:

> **I hear America singing, the varied carols I hear,**
> **Those of mechanics, each one singing his . . .**
>
> **. . . . .**
>
> **The carpenter singing his as he measures his plank or beam,**
>
> **. . . . .**
>
> **The boatman singing what belongs to him in his boat,**
> **the deckhand singing on the steamboat deck,**
> **The wood-cutter's song, the ploughboy's on his way**
> **in the morning, or at noon intermission or at sundown,**
> **The delicious singing of the mother, or the young wife at work,**
> **or of the girl sewing or washing, . . .**

There is no aristocratic vision here for the poet. It is an optimistic statement of faith in the wholesomeness of the nation and its people - a people whose "varied carols," work songs and lullabies, rise like a national anthem of praise to the poet's ear. The value of the individual is not lost to Whitman. The single voice, personal and unique, important to the poet; each person has his own integrity and worth:

> Each singing what belongs to him or her and to none
> else, . . .

THE PROPHETIC VOICE

In "Eidolons" Whitman creates a tone of prophetic mysticism:

> I met a seer,
> Passing the hues and objects of the world,
> The fields of art and learning, pleasure, sense,
> To glean eidolons.

Eidolon is a Greek word meaning an image, phantom, or spector. Whitman intends the word to stand for his idea of a spiritual form of "soul" lying behind the physical appearances of the material world:

> Beyond thy lectures learn'd professor,
> Beyond thy telescope or spectroscope observer keen,
> beyond all mathematics,
>
> . . . . .
>
> The entities of entities, eidolons.

The seer's message concerns the spiritual - the ideal forms or essences behind physical objects. All things in the world, "oceans . . . rivers . . . woman, man, or state," possess a spiritual dimension; and each is a portion of the great "soul" of nature and the universe. The eidolons endure as the material world progresses through its cycle of creation, decay, and rebirth. Therefore, eidolons constitute the true reality for Whitman:

> Ever the mutable,
> Ever materials, changing, crumbling, re-cohering,
>
> . . . . .
>
> **Issuing eidolons.**

Whitman looks prophetically ahead with a consciousness of the eternal quality of the eidolons, linking the present to the future:

> **Unfix'd yet fix'd,**
> **Ever shall be, ever have been and are,**
> **Sweeping the present to the infinite future,**
> **Eidolons, eidolons, eidolons.**

The poet then extends this conception of spiritual images, or essences inhabiting the material world, to an identification of what he believes "self" to be. In the first "Inscription," Whitman declared: "One's-Self I sing." In "Eidolons" he asserts that "self" is more than the bodily form of a person:

> **Thy body permanent,**
> **The body lurking there within thy body,**
> **The only purport of the form thou art, the real I myself,**
> **An image, an eidolon.**

For Whitman, the "real I myself" is the spiritual image or form behind the physical appearance - it is the eidolon.

SUMMARY

Filled with a lyrical flavor that is both mystical and earthly, the *Inscriptions* are much like advertisements for the poetry that lies ahead. Here Whitman establishes the general order that he will follow and outlines the scope of his poetry: the human body in all its aspects; the consideration of "self" as an individual and in relation to humanity; the glorification of the common man, of nature, of America and its democracy. The poet is both confident and prophetic. He pays homage to the past, yet his eyes are optimistically upon the future. His vision of America is charged with an enthusiasm for her people and for the physical and social energy of a growing democracy. Whitman believes that pure spiritual forms (eidolons) exist behind the material appearances of all things. He is confident of the physical and spiritual order in the universe and the importance of "Modern Man" in it. "The Modern Man I sing," writes Whitman; and he pledges to examine him in a new way:

Pressing the pulse of the life that has seldom exhibited Itself, (the great pride of man in himself,) Chanter of Personality, outlining what is yet to be, I project the history of the future. "To a Historian"

STARTING FROM PAUMANOK

BACKGROUND

"Starting from Paumanok" is one of the two most autobiographical poems in *Leaves of Grass*; the other is "Song of Myself." In the poem the personal voice of the poet blends with the broad, more representative persona. In the opening lines of "Paumanok", we are given straight biography by Whitman:

> **Starting from fish-shaped Paumanok where I was born,**
> **Well-begotten, and rais'd by a perfect mother,**
> **After roaming many lands, lover of populous pavements,**
> **Dweller in Manahatta my city, or on southern savannas, . . .**

Whitman was born on Paumanok (Long Island), of good ancestry and a good mother. It will be recalled that he had lived and worked in the New York area (Manahatta my city), and that at one time he journeyed south to be an editor of a New Orleans newspaper (southern savannas). However, Whitman adds a more universal personality to his character. Poetically, be becomes many men in many places; he had done everything and has seen everything:

Or a soldier camp'd or carrying my knapsack and gun, or a
miner in California,
Or rude in my home in Dakota's woods, my diet meat, my drink from the spring,
Or withdrawn to muse and meditate in some deep recess,
Far from the clank of crowds intervals passing rapt and happy,
Aware of the fresh free giver the flowing Missouri, aware
of mighty Niagara,
Aware of the buffalo herds grazing the plains, the hirsute
and strong-breasted bull,
Of earth, rocks, Fifth-month flowers experienced, stars,
rain, snow, my amaze,
Having studied the mocking-bird's tones and the flight of
the mountain-hawk,
And heard at dusk the unrivall'd one, the hermit thrush
from the swamp-cedars,
Solitary, singing in the West, I strike up for a New World.

APPEAL TO THE SENSES

It is very difficult to read a section of Whitman's poetry, such as the one above and not be aware of the energy that races through it. This is not uncommon in Whitman's verse, and examples of an almost electric enthusiasm of the poet for his subject can be discovered throughout *Leaves of Grass*. In such a "catalogue" of experience as this, it can be seen that Whitman's poetry is very "sensuous." This means that there is an appeal to the senses in the writing - seeing, hearing, touching, etc. The poet appeals to the sense of taste with his "diet meat" and his "drink from the spring." The reader's sense of hearing is aroused by the "clank of crowds" and becomes keener with the beautiful song of "the hermit thrush from the swamp-cedars" and "the mocking-bird's tones." We can see with Whitman the soaring "flight of the mountain hawk" and the lazy "buffalo herds grazing the plains." Such an intensive sensuous appeal on the part of the poet makes the images seem almost real to the reader. Whitman wants his audience to experience as closely as possible his enthusiasm and the sense of intimacy with nature that is such an essential part of *Leaves of Grass*.

THE VISIONARY

After literally starting from Paumanok, Whitman defies time and distance and enters what appears to be a dreamlike world of visions and ideas. He becomes the visionary, detached from his mid-nineteenth century America and conscious of life, nations, people, societies, and the world itself as parts of a great evolutionary process:

> **Then this is life,**
> **Here is what has come to the surface after so many throes and convulsions.**

The poet views the world as a whole from a distance, seeing before him a vast map of continents:

> **See the revolving globe,**

> The ancestor-continents away group'd together,
> The present and future continents north and south, with the isthmus between.

Whitman's gaze was momentarily upon the old world, but he is drawn to a vision of the growing new world and the grand panorama of American development:

> See, the vast trackless spaces,
> As in a dream they change, they swiftly fill,
> Countless masses debouch upon them,
> They are now covered with the foremost people, arts, institutions, known.
>
> . . . . .
>
> With firm and regular step they wend, they never stop,
> Successions of men, Americanos, a hundred millions,
> . . .

THE POET-PROPHET

The nineteenth-century English writer Thomas Carlyle wrote that "Literary men are . . . a perpetual priesthood." The ideal poet was to Carlyle a combination of priest-prophet-leader. Whitman takes on something of this appearance as he assumes his persona in "Starting from Paumanok":

> For me an audience interminable.
>
> . . . . .

> With faces turn'd sideways or backward towards me
> to listen,
> With eyes retrospective towards me.
> Americanos! conquerers! ...
> For you a programme of chants.

Here, Whitman has assumed the proportions of a national spokesman. His persona is that of a poet-messiah and the herald of a growing America and its people:

> Whoever you are, to you endless announcements!
> Daughter of the lands did you wait for your poet?
> Did you wait for one with a flowing mouth and
> indicative hands?
> Toward the male of the States, and toward the female
> of the State?
> Exulting words, words to Democracy's lands.

The direction of "Starting from Paumanok" is toward the future, but Whitman acknowledges that the present and future are always fed by knowledge from the past:

> Dead poets, philosophs, priests,
> Martyrs, artists, inventors, governments long since,
>
> . . . . .
>
> I dare not proceed till I respectfully credit what you
> have left wafted hither,
> I have perused it, own it is admirable, (moving awhile
> among it,)
> Think nothing can ever be greater, nothing can ever
> deserve more than it deserves, . . .

Whitman is the poet of the new blossoming America. His poetry and the **themes** it contains are new, distinct, and unique; they are not bound to the past by any ties stronger than those of respect.

I stand in my place with my own day here.

CATALOGUES AND REPETITIONS

When reading "Starting from Paumanok," we become aware of two literary devices that the poet uses repeatedly throughout *Leaves of Grass*. The first device is the "catalogue." This term refers to the long lists of cities, states, rivers, people, occupations, or objects with which he fills his verse. The following Whitman catalogue of Indian tribes is an example of this device:

The red aborigines,

. . . . .

Okonee, Koosa, Ottawa, Monongahela, Sauk, Natchez, Chattahoochee, Kaqueta, Oronoco, Wabash, Miami, Saginaw, Chippewa, Oshkosh, Walla-Walla, . . .

The second device that Whitman uses very frequently is "repetition." By repeating a word or phrase over and over, an emphasis and dramatic buildup can be achieved. "Starting from Paumanok" supplies an excellent example of this convention:

O camerado close! O you and me at last, and us two only.
O a word to clear one's path ahead endlessly!

O something ecstatic and undemonstratable! O music wild!
O now I triumph - and you shall also;
O hand in hand - O wholesome pleasure -
O one more desirer and lover!
O to haste firm holding - to haste, haste on with me.

GOOD AND EVIL

When *Leaves of Grass* was first published in 1855, it was received for the most part with uncomprehending silence by the public. What outspoken public reaction there was consisted of shock and indignation. The *Christian Examiner* of November 1856 remarked that it was "bound in conscience" to call the book "impious and obscene ... an affront upon the recognized morality of respectable people." The book was, they added, "a work that teems with abominations." The frank presentation of sexual **imagery**, normal and abnormal, and the poet's failure to distinguish between good and evil, jolted an audience accustomed to the moderation of traditional "good taste" in literature. If we consider Whitman's *Inscriptions* as 'blueprints' for the rest of *Leaves of Grass*, we are aware that the poet's intention is to range over the whole expanse of life, personal and universal. If he is to do this, he cannot choose and discard according to what is good and what is evil, according to what flatters the public taste and what appalls it. Good and evil are parts of life's whole and, as such, are a part of the entire human experience that falls within his poetic gaze. All facets of life - the people, the nation, the material world, the reader, and even Whitman himself - contain this balance of good and evil within them. Whitman is celebrating the "self," the individual and society, democratic America, and at times even the universe. To do so properly, he must include the faults along with the perfections. In "Starting from Paumanok," he makes a full statement of this intention:

> Omnes! Omnes! let others ignore what they may
> I make the poem of evil, I commemorate that part also,
> I am myself just as much evil as good, and my nation is -
> and I say there is in fact no evil,
> (Or if there is I say it is just as important to you, to the
> land or to me, as any thing else.)

He makes no moral judgments; to do so would be to break faith with his poetic intention and narrow the great width of his gaze. When Whitman considers the idea of "evil" at all, he regards it as just another part of existence. Whitman sees only the optimistic side of life with promise and hope in all things. It is not that he believes that "out of evil cometh good," for he actually denies the very existence of evil. He is concerned with the positive side of things, and whatever exists as a part of life and reality cannot be unwholesome for him in its nature:

> And I will show you that there is no imperfection in the
> present, and can be none in the future,
> And I will show that whatever happens to anybody it
> may be turn'd to beautiful results, . . .

All things, all reality, all conditions have an ultimate good in Whitman's eyes:

> And I will show you that nothing can happen more
> beautiful than death,
>
> . . . . .

**And that all the things of the universe are perfect miracles,
each as profound as any.**

All of life and reality, now and in the future, enjoy Whitman's full confidence and represent, in their parts and in unison, examples of perfection for the poet.

THE BODY AND THE SOUL

In "Starting from Paumanok," Whitman particularizes some of the broad notions of matter and spirit that he presented in "Eidolons." For Whitman, the eidolon was the spiritual form or image lying behind the physical appearances of things. "Starting from Paumanok" intensifies his ideas regarding the intimacy of matter and soul:

**And I will not make a poem nor the least part of a poem
but has reference to the soul,
Because having look'd at the objects of the universe,
I find
there is no one nor any particle of one but has reference
to the soul.**

For Whitman, the soul made itself apparent "only through matter." Therefore, it is understandable that the human body and the material world would occupy a position of great importance for him:

I will make poems of materials, for I think they are to be

**the most spiritual poems,
And I will make the poems of my body and of mortality, . . .**

Reference to the human body and to any of its functions in his poetry was perfectly reasonable to Whitman. In addition to the shock value that such topics possessed, their inclusion in his verse was in keeping with the poet's broad plan in *Leaves of Grass*. As we have seen, Whitman did not profess any traditional belief in the existence of evil. If he acknowledged evil at all, it was only as a single part of life itself and therefore as equal to the other parts:

In "Starting from Paumanok," body and soul lose their separateness and distinctness and blend into an actual identification with one another:

**Behold, the body includes and is the meaning, the main
concern, and includes and is the soul;
Whoever you are, how superb and how divine is your body,
or any part of it!**

The idea of a world-soul, or great-soul-of-nature, and the intimacy and identification of body with soul, converge in "Starting from Paumanok." The following lines reveal this mystical attitude of Whitman's:

**Was somebody asking to see the soul?
See, your own shape and countenance, persons, substances,
beasts, the trees, the running rivers, the rocks and sands.**

**All hold spiritual joys and afterwards loosen them;
How can the real body ever die and be buried?**

This identification of the body with the spiritual in Whitman's poetry gives the body a grand purity and value - nothing about it could really be offensive. On one occasion, before Whitman had composed *Leaves of Grass*, he observed in a notebook entry that he would agree to the superiority of the spiritual over the material, "When I see where the east is greater than the west."

SUMMARY

In "Starting from Paumanok," the Whitman persona broadens through visions of the old world and the new. Whitman's verse is flowing and sensuous. He speaks optimistically as a poet-prophet, with the attention of his American audience turned toward him. The poet is not concerned with conventional notions of good and evil, for he believes that all facets of life are important and have ultimate value. "Starting from Paumanok" contains Whitman's ideas on the intimacy of body and soul, an intimacy which elevates the body to the level of the spiritual and identifies the one with the other.

Whitman wished to have his own life reflected in *Leaves of Grass*. Many of the biographical elements seen in "Starting from Paumanok" are examples of this effort to preserve his own presence in the poetry.

Inscriptions lacks any real unity; Whitman's ideas appear scattered. "Starting from Paumanok," besides advancing the development of the themes, unifies the poet's thought and brings together the loosely strung ideas of *Inscriptions* into a single poem.

SONG OF MYSELF

TEXTUAL ANALYSIS

SECTIONS 1-16

BACKGROUND

It has been mentioned previously that "Song of Myself" is one of the two strongly personal and autobiographical poems in *Leaves of Grass*. However, the poem as it appeared in the first edition of 1855 was untitled and did not possess the intense personal expression of later editions. The personality it revealed was closer to that of a robust poet-herald than to that of Walt Whitman, the individual. As subsequent editions appeared, various lines and passages were added to or eliminated from the text; these alterations led the bold voice in the poetry and the personality of its author along converging paths. From its original untitled condition, the work became "A Poem of Walt Whitman, an American," then simply "Walt Whitman." In 1881 the poet established "Song of Myself" as the final title. It should be remembered that the group of poems called *Inscriptions* and the single poem "Starting from Paumanok" did not appear in the 1855 edition. Their composition and unification as a group and as a long single poem did not occur until alter. "Song of Myself" appeared at the beginning of the anonymously published book of verse as an inventory of **themes** without the clean direction contained in *Inscriptions* or the even bolder assertions of the "Paumanok" poem. While a prose preface to the first edition of *Leaves of Grass* asserted much of the poet's intention, it could not provide the necessary poetic growth and movement of thought leading into "Song of Myself," even though it was clustered and thickly populated with ideas and sensations. The excursion into "Song of Myself" required a poetically artistic preparation. When many of the ideas found in the 1855 preface materialized in *Inscriptions* and in "Paumanok," the proper avenue of entry was provided. Whitman's first-edition version of "Song of Myself" lacked the system of numbered divisions upon which he later settled. The final organization presented a poem divided into fifty-two sections and containing 1,346 lines. Between 1855 and the final arrangement in 1892, Whitman struck out many lines and added many others. Despite revisions of forty-three years, the final version contained but ten lines more than did the original form of the poem. As many critics have observed, it appears that Whitman may have altered his attitude toward his themes; but he never altered their essential integrity. His revisions of "Song of Myself" seem to point up his ability to be flexible within closely thought-out boundaries.

SECTIONS 1-4

Whitman begins "Song of Myself" in a tone of boastful authority that seems to point a finger and turn the listeners' complacent attention directly toward the poet:

> **I celebrate myself, and sing myself,**
> **And what I assume you shall assume,**

> For every atom belonging to me as good belongs to you.

Whitman is once again asserting the notion of self and its identification with all selves, as well as emphasizing his belief in the interrelationship of all beings and all matter. Whitman's tendency, in later editions, to bring himself personally into the poem can be seen in the following addition to **Section 1**:

> My tongue, every atom of my blood, form'd from this soil, this air,
> Born here of parents born here from parents the same,
> and their parents the same,
> I, now thirty-seven years old in perfect health begin,
> Hoping to cease not till death.

When we search for unity in these sections, a thread of strong physical experience and sensuous gratification is evident. Examples of this are:

> Houses and rooms are full of perfumes, the shelves are crowded with perfumes,
> I breathe the fragrance myself and know it and like it,
>
> . . . . .
>
> The atmosphere is not a perfume, it has no taste of the distillation, it is odorless,
>
> . . . . .
>
> I am mad for it to be in contact with me.

. . . . .

My respiration and inspiration, the beating of my
heart, . . .
The sniff of green leaves and dry leaves, . . .

. . . . .

The sound of belch'd words of my voice loos'd to the
eddies of the wind,
A few light kisses, a few embraces, a reaching around
of arms,

. . . . .

My dinner, dress, associates, looks, compliments,
dues,

. . . . .

The sickness of one of my folks or of myself, . . .

SECTION 5

Toward the end of **Section 4**, Whitman begins to slow the pace of his poetry. **Section 4** terminates with:

I have no mocking or arguments, I witness and wait.

There is an atmosphere of pause that hangs on the edge of expectancy. For the moment, the poet has turned away from his frantic tumble through experience and sensation. In **Section 5**, he calmly but directly addresses the soul and invites a spiritual communion:

> I believe in you my soul, . . .
>
> . . . . .
>
> Loafe with me on the grass, loose the stop
> from your throat, . . .

In an expression of personal faith, Whitman says:

> And I know that the hand of God is the promise of
> my own,
> And I know that the spirit of God is the brother of
> my own,
> And that all the men ever born are also my brothers,
> and the women my sisters and lovers,
> And that a kelson of the creation is love,
> And limitless are leaves stiff or drooping in the fields,
> And brown ants in the little wells beneath them, . . .

There is a harmonious union here. The poet professes a relationship with his deity that is closer to the idea of spiritual fraternity and partnership than to the more traditional religious notions of man's humility before a "Supreme Being."

For the individual, there is a brotherhood with all other humans that is bound together by love, a "kelson," a unifying and strengthening force. Every man and woman, every scattered leaf, and even the unnoticed ant have their place with a special importance in the universe.

SECTION 6

The notion of unity and interrelationship between all things in the world provides a transition for Whitman to his mystical impression of the grass. For Whitman, the grass is not simply a separate and distinct growth but is part of all things. It has an identity with them and represents their unity and transformation from one form to another in a cycle of life, death, and rebirth:

>A child said What is the grass? . . .
>
>. . . . .
>
>I guess it must be the flag of my disposition, . . .
>Or I guess it is the handkerchief of the Lord,
>
>. . . . .
>
>Or I guess the grass is itself a child, the produced babe of the vegetation.
>
>. . . . .
>
>And now it seem to me the beautiful uncut hair of graves.
>
>. . . . .
>
>It may be you transpire from the breasts of young men,
>
>. . . . .
>
>It may be you are from old people, or from offspring

> taken soon out of their mothers' laps.
> And here you are the mothers' laps.

Whitman's notion of life and death does not follow the more orthodox religions in which a conscious and purely spiritual existence is lived after a mortal life span. We have seen that spirit and matter are identical for Whitman; death for him does not represent any break or halting in the flow of life. If matter goes on, then life and the spirit go on. In the idea of reincarnation, there is a sense of continuity and deep satisfaction for the poet:

> What do you think has become of the young and old men?
> And what do you think has become of the women and children?
> They are alive and well somewhere,
> The smallest sprout shows there is really no death,
> And if ever there was it led forward life, and does not wait at the end to arrest it,
> And ceas'd the moment life appear'd.

The infinite, eternally sprouting grass is both the symbol and a functioning part of Whitman's forward regenerating movement of all life:

> All goes onward and outward, nothing collapses,
> And to die is different from what any one supposed, and luckier.

SECTION 7

The sections of "Song of Myself" are not totally isolated and unconnected. However, the order of their development is not necessarily consecutive; a particular idea found in one section may not be developed until several sections later. Very often, the end of one section can be found to contain an idea, phrase, or even world that is picked up by the succeeding one and carried on to fuller development. **Section 7** commences by expanding Whitman's last statement in **Section 6**, that death is actually appealing and that it is fortunate, even "lucky," to die:

> **Has any one supposed it lucky to be born?**
> **I hasten to inform him or her it is just as lucky to die, and I know it.**

In Whitman's philosophy, birth and death are not poles apart: they are links in a chain. One life leads into a death, and that death touches upon a next life, in infinite succession. In Whitman's universe there is a perpetual process of change occurring, beneath which is the constant factor - the soul. Death, in the traditional sense, brings about only a reforming or reshaping of matter and soul. The ideas of reincarnation and transmigration (the movement of the soul from one body to a succeeding one upon death) have the excitement of a great adventure for Whitman. They imply a desirable impatience for death on his part, not unlike that contained in the deep spirituality of many religions.

For Whitman, birth is not the one beginning, and death is not the final end. Existence is not a few short years pressed in between life and death. It represents something of an infinite line along which occur an infinite series of births, deaths, and rebirths for every individual. There is no death, as such; all things continue as part of the material and spiritual integrity and development of the universe.

In **Section 7**, the poet mystically contemplates life, death, and the infinite forward movement of matter and spirit, preparing to thrust himself into an excursion,

> **And peruse manifold objects, no two alike and every one good,**
>
> **. . . . .**
>
> **Undrape! you are not guilty to me, nor stale nor discarded, . . .**

There is wholesomeness and perfection in every person, object, and facet of life. For Whitman, the damaging effects of opinion, time, and disuse are of little importance; the essential goodness of all things radiates for him.

SECTIONS 8-10

Whitman plunges into a wild gallop through long catalogues so thickly populated with people, places, occupations, objects, and animals, that they suggest the density, infinity, and overall oneness of Whitman's mystical "grass" itself. The poetic voice now has a boundless energy and capacity for seeing and being all things. We must keep in mind the poet's idea of material and spiritual unity in the world, as we read through the enormous span of sight and experience that appears to roll on endlessly:

> **The little one sleeps in its cradle,**
>
> **. . . . .**

The suicide sprawls on the bloody floor of the bedroom,

. . . . .

The dried grass of the harvest-time loads the slow-drawn wagon,

. . . . .

I am there, I help, I came stretch'd atop the load,

. . . . .

The boatman and clam-diggers arose early and stopt for me,

. . . . .

The runaway slave came to my house and stopt outside,

. . . . .

I had him sit next me at table, my fire-lock lean'd in the corner.

SECTION 11

For three sections Whitman expands his poetic persona over an expanse of robust and masculine experience. Suddenly there is a change of focus in time, location, and even gender. **Section 11** reveals the erotic gaze and reaction of a woman watching young men bathing. She watches them in secret from her window:

> **Twenty-eight years of womanly life and all so lonesome.**
>
> . . . . .
>
> **Ah the homeliest of them is beautiful to her.**

The passage is sharply sensual and requires a quick refocus of the reader's attention. Its sudden appearance is somewhat startling, but it is not included by Whitman merely for flexible pace. He is the "poet of the body" as well as of the soul. In *Inscriptions*, he acknowledged that:

> **The Female equally with the Male I sing.**

As the woman and her sexual longings are concealed behind the curtains of her window the openly erotic in *Leaves of Grass* has appeared but fleetingly, with a hinted explosive force just beneath the surface. Whitman has not yet freely opened this dimension of the self. **Section 11** is a forerunner of the intensely sexual poetry that will be met later in the *Children of Adam* and *Calamus* sections.

SECTION 12

Whitman once again takes up his fantastic excursion, in almost brutal contrast to the effeminacy of the preceding passage. The masculine quality of the section betrays a touch of strong sensuality in the poetic voice of the observer:

> Blacksmiths with grimed and hairy chests environ the anvil,
> Each has his main-sledge, they are all out, there is a great heat in the fire.
> From the cinder-strew'd threshold I follow their movements,
> The lith sheer of their waists plays even with their massive arms,
> Overhand the hammers swing, overhand so slow, overhand so sure,
> They do not hasten, each man hits in his place.

In these last two lines, there is a feeling of continuity and pattern: a slow, unchanging process not unlike Whitman's overall concept in which each part and aspect of life and the universe has its own individual and valuable function.

SECTION 13

In this section, lurking sensuality is present once again. Whitman curiously augments masculine description with qualities that are somewhat feminine, and this only intensifies the **realism** of the image:

> The Negro . . .
>
> . . . . .
>
> His blue shirt exposes his ample neck and breast . . .
>
> . . . . .
>
> The sun . . . falls on the black of his polish'd

and perfect limbs.

This section also contains a statement of the poet's function on this wide journey through time and space. In fact, it is a statement of the poet's function and purpose throughout *Leaves of Grass* as a whole:

> In me the caresser of life wherever moving, backward as well as forward sluing,
> To niches aside and junior bending, not a person or object missing,
> Absorbing all to myself and for this song.

The "caresser of life" meditates on the mysteries of life and creation which emanate from even the most uninspired of beasts:

> Oxen that rattle the yoke and chain or halt in the leafy shade, what is that you express in your eyes?
> It seems to me more than all the print I have read in my life.

The plan and order of the universe is evident in the beasts and birds of the fields, and the poet-traveller sees order and design in the work of creation. The "wood-drake" and "wood-duck" are flushed from cover at his approach:

> I believe in those wing'd purposes,
> And acknowledge red, yellow, white, playing within me,
> And consider green and violet and the tufted crown intentional, . . .

The colors and the truths of nature are "playing within" the chanting voice. There is more than mere observation present: the voice is a part of the very things it describes and experiences so movingly.

SECTION 14

In this section, the poet moves toward an understanding of his own place in the order of things. He does this by means of an intimate understanding of the place held by the animals in nature's pattern:

> **The wild gander leads his flock through the cool night,**
> **Ya-honk he says, and sounds it down to me like an invitation,**
> **The pert may suppose it meaningless, but I listening close,**
> **Find its purpose and place up there toward the wintry sky.**

In observing the "sharp-hoof'd moose," the "grunting sow," and the "brood of the turkey-hen," the "caresser of life" beholds in the governing order and forces of the universe a pattern in which he too is a part:

> **I see in them and myself the same old law.**

This "same old law" permeates the whole of *Leaves of Grass*. It contains Whitman's attitudes toward reincarnation and the transmigration of the soul that we have seen previously. It also involves notions we might identify as pantheism, a philosophy which, in general, sees the material world as one and the same with God. Creation for the pantheist is not merely the handiwork of a creator; it is really the substance of the creator itself. "Itself" is a better word to use than "Himself" when considering Whitman's pantheism, for his God is not one of personality; nor is it a deity in the traditional Christian or Hebraic sense.

It will be recalled that in **Section 5** Whitman stated:

And I know that the hand of God is the promise of my own,
And I know that the spirit of God is the brother of my own,. . .

In the Judeo-Christian sense, this attitude is unacceptable, for it places the created on a par with the Creator. For Whitman, it is an exciting creed; for in it there is the great union of all created things, a oneness of matter and spirit, and a participation in the divine nature of all creation. Thus, in the "old law" the poet shares in the identity of all other life, as well as in that which he recognizes as God. All creation and the innumerable people, objects, experiences, and sensations have real value to him and are a constant reminder of the laws which he believes govern the universe. The "grass" of the book's title is a pantheistic grass for the poet. It represents, and is a recurring symbol of, that recurring "same old law" throughout the poetry.

SECTION 15

This body of verse contains great catalogues of people and their work. Almost every line is a quick by striking "slice of life." Whitman presses together a thick cross section of humanity, yet none of his deft sketches appears in any way fuzzy or poorly defined. We can distinguish each clearly from the rest of the crowd that stands by it shoulder to shoulder. Much of the success in a catalogue such as this is the diversity of Whitman's selective eye. Criticism has been directed at the poet for lack of discrimination in selecting the components of many of his catalogues. It has been remarked that the contents cannot be justified over other possible selections. This may be true; however, to attack parts is not necessarily to undermine successfully the merits of the whole. Whitman's catalogues may appear billowy and the contents overabundant; nevertheless, his eye is keyed to variety and contrast, and on these qualities rest the strength of the catalogues' total impression and the sharpness of **imagery** obtainable within the space of one or two lines. The strong contrasts in subject and tone serve to isolate each fleeting vision without destroying the integrity of the entire panorama. A careful comparison of the characters included reveals that the selection was not careless. Each of Whitman's figures is distinct. He has the ability to explode detail into significant matter for the eye and ear:

The married and unmarried children ride home to their Thanksgiving dinner,

. . . . .

The deacons are ordained with cross'd hands at the altar,

. . . . .

The farmer stops by the bars as he walks on a First-day
loafe and looks at the oats and rye,

. . . . .

> The quadroon girl is sold at the auction-stand, the drunkard nods by the bar-room stove,
>
> . . . . .
>
> The youth lies awake in the cedar-roof'd garret and harks to the musical rain,
>
> . . . . .
>
> The connoisseur peers along the exhibition-gallery with halfshut eyes bent sideways, . . .

A Whitman glimpse of life is usually all the more striking because of the boldly contrasting members of the catalogue that precede and follow it directly. A "bride" and an "opium-eater," a "prostitute" and a "President" - Whitman's democratic catalogues never permit class distinction:

> The bride unrumples her white-dress, the minute-hand
> of the clock moves slowly,
> The opium-eater reclines with rigid head and just-open'd lips,
> The prostitute draggles her shawl, her bonnet bobs on
> her tipsy and pimpled neck,
>
> . . . . .
>
> The President holding his cabinet council is surrounded
> by the great Secretaries, . . .

As the poet rushes ahead through his dense vision of humanity, his recording eye often becomes tender and sympathetic. In what are almost stage whispers, he mellows the bold **realism** of what he sees with the understanding of the "caresser of life," loving humanity and feeling compassion for its situation. Of the young wagon driver, Whitman remarks:

... **(I love him, though I do not know him;)** ...

To the prostitute amid the anguish of public torment, Whitman extends the fullness of pity and divine love:

(Miserable! I do not laugh at your oaths nor jeer you;) ...

Toward the end of **Section 15**, the swift movement of the passage tapers to the peace and slumber of a day's end and a quiet philosophic overtone:

The city sleeps and the country sleeps,
The living sleep for their time, the dead sleep for their time, ...

The deceleration of the passage becomes complete as the poet unifies his experience, relating it to himself and to the broad plan of his poetry:

And such as it is to be of these more or less I am,
And of these one and all I weave the song of myself.

During the previous sections, Whitman's conception of "self" has expanded from the declaration in **Section 1**,

I celebrate myself, and sing myself,

to a wide, mystical awareness of a diversity of "self" that includes, and is, all people and all things, of all degrees and all kinds. The "I" of the poet has become the "Omnes! omnes!" of "Starting from Paumanok," and his "programme of chants" brings him from intimacy to a fuller identification with all creation. He is mystically conscious of both the part and the whole in the great order of the universe:

> **(The moth and the fish-eggs are in their place,**
> **The bright suns I see and the dark suns I cannot see are in their place,**
> **The palpable is in its place and the impalpable in its place.)**

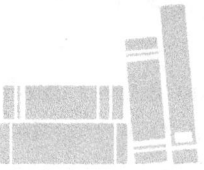

SONG OF MYSELF

TEXTUAL ANALYSIS

SECTIONS 17-38

SECTION 17

A pause of transition and contemplation occurs in **Section 17**. The poet remarks upon the eternal quality in all that he has experienced:

> **These are really the thoughts of all men in all ages and lands,**
> **they are not original with me, . . .**

Whitman then returns to the symbol of the mystical grass and couples it with an element equally as diffuse and endless:

> **This is the grass that grows wherever the land is and the water is,**
> **This is the common air that bathes the globe.**

Repeatedly, Whitman weaves into his poetry notions of the equality and unity of all things against the background of the universal and eternal. The constancy of an evolutionary pattern works its way from one end of *Leaves of Grass* to the other. The recurring image of the "grass" symbolizes in its vastness a unity of many parts, while its limitless "organic" growth accords with the living and growing creative quality of Whitman's poetry. The joining of the "grass" image with that of the "common air" intensifies the commonness, equality, and universality already associated with the infinite "grass."

SECTION 18

Commencing with **Section 18**, Whitman once again confronts the diversity of humanity - not with the soaring overview of the fast - paced catalogues, but by reaching down to the shadows where the forgotten, defeated and rejected can be found. There is a triumphal and marshaling tone to the poet's song and what might be called the negative members of humanity find approval in the resurrecting cry of the poet's voice:

> **With music strong I come, with my coronets and my drums,**
> **I play not marches for accepted victors only, I play marches for conquer'd and slain persons.**
>
> . . . . .
>
> **Vivas to those who have fail'd!**
>
> . . . . .
>
> **And the numberless unknown heroes equal to the**

greatest heroes known!

SECTION 19

Whitman's visitation of the blighted contains a call to justification and integrity, not in the Christian religious sense of divine mercy and forgiveness from without, but on the grounds of an internal wholesomeness more essential than the accidents of circumstances. In **Section 19**, the poet identifies the members of his "Omnes! omnes!" and promises to exclude no one:

> **This is the meal equally set, this the meat for natural hunger,**
> **It is for the wicked just the same as the righteous,**
> **I make appointments with all,**
> **I will not have a single person slighted or left away,**
> **The kept-woman, sponger, thief, are hereby invited,**
> **The heavy-lipp'd slave is invited, the venerealee is invited;**
> **There shall be no difference between them and the rest.**

And for the poet, there is "no difference between them" and him:

> **This the touch of my lips to yours, this the murmur of yearning,**
> **This the far-off depth and height reflecting my own face,**
> **This the thoughtful merge of myself, and the outlet again.**

SECTION 20

Whitman now asks:

> What is a man anyhow? what am I? what are you?

His response to his own question is brash and arrogant, with an independent and self-satisfied air:

> I wear my hat as I please indoors or out.
> Why should I pray? why should I venerate and be ceremonious?

> . . . . .

> I find no sweeter fat than stick to my own bones.

> . . . . .

> I exist as I am, that is enough,

> . . . . .

> I laugh at what you call dissolution,
> And I know the amplitude of time.

The egotism that seems to leap out of these lines is best understood in the context of Whitman's broad notion of "self." As an individual, he is part of all he symbolizes:

> In all people I see myself, none more and not one a barley-corn less,
> And the good or bad I say of myself I say of them.

Whitman is a poet bringing the promise of immortality. It is with immortality in mind that he can strut so arrogantly his ideas of "man" and "self," which are, at the same time, both personal and universal:

> **I know I am deathless,**
> **I know this orbit of mine cannot be swept by**
> **a carpenter's compass,**
> **I know I shall not pass like a child's curlicue cut**
> **with a burnt stick at night.**
>
> **. . . . .**
>
> **I see that the elementary laws never apologize,**
>
> **. . . . .**
>
> **One world is aware and by far the largest to me,**
> **and that is myself,**
> **And whether I come to my own to-day or in ten**
> **thousand**
> **or ten million years,**
> **I can cheerfully take it now, or with equal cheerfulness**
> **I can wait.**

This is the reason why the poet can "laugh" at "dissolution"; he is conscious of a great process of regeneration and evolution, "the elementary laws" in "the amplitude of time."

SECTION 21

There is a pattern of recurrence in the appearance of Whitman's themes. The poet allows an idea to work its way to the surface periodically, at times stated and undeveloped, on other occasions expanded and given more shape and substance. In **Section 21**, Whitman commences by measuring out his verse with the tone and pace of a Biblical psalmist:

> **I am the poet of the Body and I am the poet of the Soul,**
> **The pleasures of heaven are with me and the pains of hell**
> **are with me,**
> **The first I graft and increase upon myself, the latter I translate into a new tongue.**

Then, of the male and the female, he says:

> **I am the poet of the woman the same as the man,**
> **And I say it is as great to be a woman as to be a man,**
> **And I say there is nothing greater than the mother of men.**

We have seen this message of the equality of body with soul and male with female previously in Whitman, and we shall encounter it again. However, in **Section 21**, the qualities usually identified with the body are transferred to nature. There is an implied division into male and female figures, and a delicate sensual texture is evoked:

> **Press close bare-bosom'd night - press close magnetic nourishing night!**
>
> . . . . .
>
> **Still nodding night - mad naked summer night.**
> **Smile O voluptuous cool-breath'd earth!**

Earth of the slumbering and liquid trees!

. . . . .

**Earth of the limpid gray of clouds brighter
and clearer for my sake!**

. . . . .

Smile, for your lover comes.

SECTION 22

The strong **imagery** of **Section 21** extends into **Section 22**, as the poet continues to "translate into a new tongue" customary associations and identifications of the passionate and erotic. The sexual **imagery** is transferred to the sea, into which the poet plunges to be absorbed in its loving embrace:

> **You sea! I resign myself to you also -
> I guess what you mean,
> I behold from the beach your crooked
> inviting fingers,
> I believe you refuse to go back without
> feeling of me,
> We must have a turn together, I undress,
> hurry me out of sight of the land,
> Cushion me soft, rock me in billowy drowse,
> Dash me with amorous wet, I can repay you.
> Sea of stretch'd ground-swells,
> Sea breathing broad and convulsive breaths, . . .**

In his union with the sea, Whitman is part of the great evolutionary and cyclic pattern of the universe.

> I am integral with you, I too am of one phase and of all phases.

As the "caresser of life," the singer of "chants" and of "Omnes! omnes!", the poet cannot exclude the land, the sea, or nature itself from his consideration; for they actually contain the endless "items" of the catalogues:

> (Shall I make my list of things in the house and
> skip the house that supports them?)

The strong sensuality of the previous passages is as proper and desirable for the poet as any other emotion:

> I am not the poet of goodness only, I do not decline
> to be the poet of wickedness also.

If such erotic pleasure is "wickedness," it is not so for Whitman, to whom all things express a natural purity. He is no moralizer and can challenge the soundness of making moral distinctions:

> What blurt is this about virtue and about vice?
> Evil propels me and reform of evil propels me,
> I stand indifferent,
> My gait is no fault-finder's or rejecter's gait,
> I moisten the roots of all that has grown.

SECTION 23

In this section, Whitman acknowledges the cyclic "wonder" and mystery of time.

> It alone is without flaw, it alone rounds and completes all, . . .

He hails "materialism" and the precise methods of the scientist:

> Hurrah for positive science! long live exact demonstration!
>
> . . . . .
>
> Gentlemen, to you the first honors always!

However, science with its precision provides no supreme answer or demonstration for the poet. The deductions of the scientist are instruments and aids leading beyond - "reminders they of life untold":

> Your facts are useful, and yet they are not my dwelling,
> I but enter by them to an area of my dwelling.

SECTION 24

The voice of the poet now returns to the chest thumping bravado of earlier sections. The boasting arrogance is here, but its tone of pride arises from a sense of common equality with all other people. The posture is that of the spokesman, arms interlocked with those he champions:

> Walt Whitman, a kosmos, of Manhattan the son,
> Turbulent, fleshy, sensual, eating, drinking and breeding,

> No sentimentalist, no stander above men and women
> or apart from them,
> No more modest than immodest.

. . . . .

> Whoever degrades another degrades me,
> And whatever is done or said returns at last to me.

. . . . .

> Through me many long dumb voices,
> Voices of the interminable generations of prisoners
> and slaves,
> Voices of the diseas'd and despairing and of
> thieves and dwarfs, . . .

A powerful spirit of purification fills these last few lines. Whitman continues to uplift the fallen and degraded of humanity:

> And of the rights of them the others are down upon,
> Of the deform'd, trivial, flat, foolish, despised, . . .

Whitman is "the poet of wickedness also," but what is wicked to the world is not evil to him. He had vowed to "translate into a new tongue," and this he does with the traditional representations of evil.

> Through me forbidden voices,
> Voices of sexes and lusts, voices veil'd
> and I remove the veil,
> Voices indecent by me clarified and transfigur'd.

Whitman reaffirms his belief in the essential integrity and goodness of all acts, sensations, and responses. The body is not to be denied, for it is equal to identifiable with the spirit:

> I do not press my finger across my mouth,
>
> . . . . .
>
> I believe in the flesh and the appetites,
>
> . . . . .
>
> Divine am I inside and out, and I make holy whatever I touch or am touch'd from,
>
> . . . . .
>
> If I worship one thing more than another it shall be the spread of my own body, or any part of it,. . .

Near the end of **Section 24**, the poet pauses to dwell a moment upon the great wonders of creation and the miracles that lie behind even the lowliest flower:

> That I walk up my stoop, I pause to consider
> if it really be,
> A morning-glory at my window satisfies me more than
> the metaphysics of books.
> To behold the day-break!
> The little light fades the immense and diaphanous shadows,
> The air tastes good to my palate.

SECTIONS 25-30

Following the mysteries and wonder of creation, Whitman prepares to examine the nature of "Being." In **Section 25**, the poet experiences the urge to spew out what he knows and what he wishes to say:

> **Walt you contain enough, why don't you let it out then?**

However, in **Section 26**, the poet's urge to express himself is replaced by passive attention:

> **Now I will do nothing but listen,**
> **To accrue what I hear into this song,**
> **to let sounds contribute toward it.**

With the tugs of expression and reception upon him, the poet commences **Section 27** with a consideration of "Being" - "the puzzle of puzzles" - and questions the nature of its identity:

> **To be in any form, what is that?**

The lowest level of "Being" would be marvelous enough for Whitman:

> **If nothing lay more develop'd the quahaug**
> **in its callous shell were enough.**

However, the poet's "Being" is more than this; it is sensitive and alive, an antenna for experience and sensation.

> **Mine is no callous shell,**
> **I have instant conductors all over me**

**whether I pass or stop,
They seize every object and lead it harmlessly through me.**

The body and its sensations are necessary for the "self" and for the awareness of "Being."

I merely stir, press, feel with my fingers, and am happy,...

With sensual exhilaration, the poet pulses with the ecstasy of touch until he cries out, no longer able to endure the sensations:

Unclench your floodgates, you are too much for me.

With this peak of erotic emotion passed, Whitman tempers his passionate outburst with philosophic observation in **Sections 29** and **30**.

All truths wait in all things,

. . . . .

The insignificant is as big to me as any,...

The body and its sense experiences are real and morally excellent to the poet; no amount of reasoning or preaching can alter that.

**(What is less or more than touch?)
Logic and sermons never convince,...**

For Whitman, the reality of sense experience cannot be denied, and, as such, "proves itself" and its wholesomeness to him.

SECTION 31

The "truths" that lie in every portion of reality, and the importance of the apparently "insignificant" to the poet, appear in **Section 31** in company with the recurring image of the "grass." The wonder of the universe is mirrored in the meanest and most common of objects and creatures.

> **I believe a leaf of grass is no less than**
> **the journey-work of the stars,**
>
> . . . . .
>
> **And a mouse is miracle enough to stagger sextillions of infidels.**

In a sprawling awareness of existence and creation, the poet seems to acquire a sure control over himself. He appears to be elevated in a soaring purity high above the great evolutionary process that he observes; yet he never loses intimate contact.

> **I find I incorporate gneiss, coal, long-threaded moss, fruits, grains, esculent roots,**
> **And am stucco'd with quadrupeds and birds all over,**
> **And have distanced what is behind me for good reasons,**
> **But call any thing back again when I desire it.**

SECTION 32

In the height of his purified state, the poet contemplates the elemental and natural integrity of birds and beasts:

> **I think I could turn and live with animals,**
> **they're so placid and self-contain'd,**
> **I stand and look at them long and long.**

The guileless and contended beast has the marks, the "tokens," of simple perfection about him:

> **They do not sweat and whine about**
> **their condition,**
> **They do not lie awake in the dark and**
> **weep for their sins,**
> **They do not make me sick discussing their**
> **duty to God, . . .**

Society has bred in men those qualities and conditions that the poet loathes; however, he no longer possesses them, since he has rid himself of society's interpretations of evil. He can turn to the animals and meditate on a purity in those creatures that is natural to them, but which required a mystical and purifying struggle for himself to obtain. However, this is no reason to elevate the beast to the level, or above the level, of man. The image of a great and powerful horse satisfies the poet's need to express the greater grandeur of man:

> **A gigantic beauty of a stallion, fresh**
> **and responsive to my caresses,**
>
> . . . . .

> I but use you a minute, then I resign you,
> stallion,
> Why do I need your paces when I myself
> out-gallop them?
> Even as I stand or sit passing faster than you.

Whitman's belief in the equality and union of all things in creation does not exclude his awareness of man's capacities and potential. The stallion is pure and magnificent; but for Whitman, man is always the perfection that forever exceeds all other perfections in creation.

SECTION 33

Through consideration of "self," "Being," the body and the soul, death, and the mysteries of existence and creation, the poet has attained an acute awareness and spiritual enlightenment. In **Section 1**, Whitman declared:

> I loafe and invite my soul,
> I lean and loafe at my ease observing
> a spear of summer grass.

Now, he penetrates the mysteries that he began to contemplate in such an easy and passionless manner.

> Space and Time! now I see it is true,
> what I guess'd at,
> What I guess'd when I loaf'd on the grass,
> What I guess'd while I lay alone in my bed,
> And again as I walk'd the beach under
> the paling stars of the morning.

Whitman then launches into an enormous catalogue of sight, sound, and experience. He appears to be in better control of his "vision" than in previous mystical flights. Having reached a point of intense and refined comprehension, he does not merely pass through his vision, but rather oversees it in an aura of all-knowing.

> **My ties and ballasts leave me,**
> **my elbows rest in seagaps,**
> **I skirt sierras, my palms over continents,**
> **I am afoot with my vision.**

In this catalogue, both "Space and Time" are overcome by the poet. In the bright inner light of his vision, he grasps details not apparent to the casual eye. Whitman experiences fresh sensations, discovers new colors and shapes in commonplace and undramatic subjects, hears the unheard sounds in the song of a bird, and, in general, sharply retains his five senses. As if seeing all the world for the first time, Whitman translates what he observes into exciting experience for the jaded and insensitive eye. His is the vision of the newborn or of the man to whom sight is suddenly given after total blindness. He has illuminated insight, and, like a skilled painter, seizes what appears to be unimportant and explodes it into wonderful significance.

> **Where heifers browse, where geese nip their food**
> **with short jerks,**
>
> . . . . .
>
> **Where the katy-did works her chromatic reed on the**
> **walnut-tree over the well,**
>
> . . . . .

> Pleas'd with the earnest words of the sweating
> Methodist preacher, . . .

> . . . . .

> By the cot in the hospital reaching lemonade to
> a feverish patient,
> Nigh the coffin'd corpse when all is still,
> examining with a candle; . . .

As a creator of animal and nature images, Whitman is masterful in **Section 33**:

> Where the mockingbird sounds his delicious gurgles,
> cackles, screams, weeps,

> . . . . .

> Where the sun down shadows lengthen over the
> limitless
> and lonesome prairie,

> . . . . .

> Where the humming-bird shimmers, where the neck
> of the
> long-lived swan is curving and winding,

From these beautiful images and from the peace of

> Walking the old hills of Judaea with the
> beautiful gentle God by my side, . . .

Whitman experiences the pain and torments that counterbalance the beauties and pleasures of life:

> My voice is the wife's voice, the screech
> by the rail of the stairs,
> They fetch my man's body up dripping and drown'd.

. . . . .

> I am the hounded slave, I wince at the bite
> of the dogs,
> Hell and despair are upon me, crack and again crack
> the marksmen, . . .

Whitman is the spokesman and spirit of all humanity in all conditions; he can declare that:

> Agonies are one of my changes of garments.

SECTIONS 34-36

These three sections contain two short tales with an American historical flavor. Alike in their settings of arms and battle, they differ in the manner in which they resolve themselves in bitterness and agony. The tale told in **Section 34** is that of the massacre of "four hundred and twelve young men" after an honorable surrender. The tale has an actual historical foundation. During the Texas revolution of 1836, Mexican forces slaughtered a band of Americans after the latter had surrendered near the town of Goliard.

Sections 35 and **36** relate the victory at sea of a sturdy "frigate" and her unconquerable captain and crew. The story has its basis in the sea engagement between John Paul Jones' vessel, the Bon Homme Richard, and the British ship Serapis, in 1779. Jones captured the British ship, but his own vessel sank, with heavy casualties on both sides.

In the "Texas" narrative, there are defeat and the agonies of massacre:

> **A few fell at once, shot in the temple or heart,**
> **the living and dead lay together,**
> **The maim'd and mangled dug in the dirt,**
> **the newcomers saw them there,**
> **Some half-kill'd attempted to crawl away,**
> **These were dispatch'd with bayonets or batter'd**
> **with the blunts of muskets, . . .**

In **Sections 35** and **36**, the fruits of John Paul Jone's triumph are as bitter as those of the conquered. The poet's lesson is a strong one: man's brutality to man in war and battle reaps a similar harvest whether in victory or in defeat. Both tales are part of the poet's great vision. They contribute authentic Americana to the poetry and participate in Whitman's impartial celebration of both the bright and dark corners of the human situation. In addition to this, they are part of the great physical and spiritual passage through which the poet journeys in *Leaves of Grass*.

SECTIONS 37-38

Whitman plunges deeper into human misery and assumes the shape and afflictions of the despairing and forsaken in life:

> For me the keepers of convicts shoulder their carbines
> and keep watch,
> It is I let out in the morning and barr'd at night.
>
> . . . . .
>
> Not a cholera patient lies at the last gasp but I also lie
> at the last gasp,
> My face is ash-color'd, my sinews gnarl,
> away from me people retreat.

The vision nearly overcomes the poet; in **Section 38**, he cries aloud:

> Enough! enough! enough!
> Somehow I have been stunn'd. Stand back!
>
> . . . . .
>
> That I could forget the mockers and insults!
> That I could forget the trickling tears and the blows of
> the bludgeons and hammers!
> That I could look with a separate look on my own
> crucifixion and bloody crowning!

The **imagery** is surely that of a Christlike lamentation and agony, but the poet quickly recovers his faith in life and the order of things:

> I troop forth replenish'd with supreme power,
> one of an average unending procession, . . .

SONG OF MYSELF

TEXTUAL ANALYSIS

SECTIONS 39-52

SECTIONS 39-40

From the trembling of the last few sections, the poet moves ahead and upward with strength and confidence. The Christ image of **Section 38** is suddenly joined by:

> The friendly and flowing savage, who is he?
> Is he waiting for civilization,
> or past it and mastering it?

The "savage" is man in his natural wholesome state, pure and uncomplicated:

> Behavior lawless as snow-flakes, words simple as grass,
> uncomb'd head, laughter, and naivete, . . .

In **Section 40**, Whitman declares suddenly:

> **Behold, I do not give lectures or a little charity,**
> **When I give I give myself.**

Three distinct personalities now converge in the poetic voice. In a curiously constructed trinity, the tender selflessness of the Christ figure and the natural unblemished simplicity of the "friendly and flowing savage" are added to the voice of the poet himself. This mixture of personalities is maintained through several lines that blend New Testament tradition with the poet's passionate love for all humanity:

> **To the cotton-field drudge or cleaner of privies I lean,**
> **On his right cheek I put the family kiss,**
> **And in my soul I swear I never will deny him.**

The Christian overtones, such as Christ's denial by the apostle Peter and the apostle Judas, are evident. However, it should be realized that the promise not to deny in these lines is not a refusal to deny a God, Christian, Hebrew, or otherwise. It is a humanitarian avowal not to deny the humblest member of the human "family." The "kiss" is the sign of that kinship and the seal of that promise.

SECTION 41

In "Starting from Paumanok," Whitman declared:

> **Dead poets, philosophs, priests,**
> **. . . . .**
> **I dare not proceed till I respectfully credit**

what you have left wafted hither, . . .

Whitman respected the past and its contributions to the long evolutionary stream of man and ideas, but he also observed:

I stand in my place with my own day here.

In **Section 41** of "Song of Myself," Whitman's faith may rise out of the creeds of the past, but it also rises above them and is superior to them:

I heard what was said of the universe,

. . . . .

It is middling well as far as it goes -
but it that all?

Whitman's faith outstrips all the old gods and religions the Hebraic and Christian God, the deities of the eastern and western worlds, the divine spirits of Scandinavia, Egypt, and of the North and South American Indian. A universality of past beliefs is climaxed in the new energetic faith of the poet:

Magnifying and applying I come,
Outbidding at the start the old cautious hucksters,
Taking myself the exact dimensions of Jehovah,

. . . . .

In my portfolio placing Manito loose, Allah on a leaf, the crucifix engraved,

**With Odin and the hideous-faced Mexitli and every idol
and image,
Taking them all for what they are worth and not a cent more,
Admitting they were alive and did the work of their days, . . .**

He secures sound principles and teachings from all creeds, for each has contributed something to the whole. Nevertheless, the sum of his impressions from them only supplies the outline for the new, rich faith that now overflows him and touches all humanity.

**Accepting the rough deific sketches to
fill out better in myself, bestowing them
freely on each man and woman I see,
Discovering as much or more in a farmer framing a house,
Putting higher claims for him there with his roll'd-up
sleeves driving the mallet and chisel, . . .**

Whitman's "religion" is more than merely tender and humanitarian. It is wildly enthusiastic about every aspect of the common man. Therefore, it might better be called a type of humanistic faith. However, it is extravagantly humanistic, since it discovers man to be as worthy of a kind of veneration as any god. Man contains "as much" and even "higher" spiritual values than the sum of all the world's religions, past and present.

SECTIONS 42-44

At the height of this profession of faith, the poet turns toward the world through which his visionary journey has conducted him. He speaks now as spokesman and spiritual leader, the prophet whose mission is to lead humanity forward.

> A call in the midst of the crowd,
> My own voice, orotund sweeping and final.
> Come my children,
> Come my boys and girls, my women,
> household and intimates, . . .

Whitman seeks to penetrate the outward appearances of things, to go beyond the product to reach the maker, behind the representation to discover that which he always values highest - man. He seeks not

> Sermons, creeds, theology - but the fathomless human brain, . . .

In **Section 43**, his message to mankind is an outpouring of the "religious" awareness that he has attained. For the poet, "religion" has the evolutionary character that he sees in the material universe; all religions, from primitive to modern, are links in a chain of development moving through time.

> Believing I shall come again upon the earth
> after five thousand years,
> Waiting responses from oracles, honoring the gods,
> saluting the sun,
>
> . . . . .

> Helping the llama or brahmin as he trims the
> lamps of the idols,
>
> . . . . .
>
> Accepting the Gospels, accepting him that was
> crucified, . . .
>
> . . . . .
>
> To the mass kneeling or the puritan's prayer rising,
> . . .

The breadth of Whitman's faith encompasses this process and incorporates, not rejects, the creeds of all ages, past and present.

> I do not despise you priests, all time,
> the world over,
> My faith is the greatest of faiths and
> the least of faiths,
> Enclosing worship ancient and modern and
> all between ancient and modern, . . .

In **Section 44**, the prophet-leader invites a contemplation of the present in relation to "eternity":

> The clock indicates the moment -
> but what does eternity indicate?
> We have thus far exhausted trillions of
> winters and summers,
> There are trillions ahead, and trillions ahead of
> them.

For Whitman, an evolutionary process is constantly pressing and carrying all humanity forward:

> The past is the push of you, me, all, precisely the same, . . .

In **Section 44** he announces that

> I am an acme of things accomplish'd,
> and I an encloser of things to be.
>
> . . . . .
>
> Immense have been the preparations for me,
>
> . . . . .
>
> Before I was born out of my mother generations guided me, . . .

The poet, as he believes each man to be, is the fruit of the past and the promise of the future.

> All forces have been steadily employ'd
> to complete and delight me,
> Now on this spot I stand with my robust soul.

SECTION 45

From the "span of youth," Whitman attains maturity:

> O manhood, balanced, florid and full.

He passes through

Old age superbly rising! O welcome, ineffable grace of dying days!

The poet contemplates the future and the fusion with "The great Camerado," the tremendous spiritual force that is Whitman's idea of deity.

**My rendezvous is appointed, it is certain,
The Lord will be there and wait
till I come on perfect terms,
The great Camerado, the lover true for
whom I pine will be there.**

It is understandable that the poet's God should be visualized as "Camerado" and "the love true." In **Section 5**, Whitman said:

And I know that the spirit of God is the brother of my own,

. . . . .

And that a kelson of the creation is love, . . .

Whitman's God has the aspect of a fraternal companion and great "lover." In the eyes of the poet, love is a strengthening fiber in the structure of creation, a necessary operating force in life.

In **Section 40**, Whitman spoke as an angel of mercy to the afflicted and wretched:

**I seize the descending man and
raise him with resistless will,**

> O despairer, here is my neck,
> By God, you shall not go down!
> hang your whole weight upon me.

However, the poet-prophet's mission is not to be a perpetual support or crutch for man. The path ahead has been opened by Whitman; and in **Section 46**, he invites the companionship of humanity:

> I tramp a perpetual journey, (come listen all!)
>
> . . . . .
>
> But each man and each woman of you I lead upon a knoll,
> My left hand hooking you round the waist,
> My right hand pointing to landscapes of continents and the public road.

Man must rely on himself and be self-sufficient. Whitman's philosophy maintains that self-dependence is a condition that is indispensable for man.

> Shoulder your duds dear son, and I will mine, and let us hasten forth,
>
> . . . . .
>
> You are also asking me questions and I hear you,
> I answer that I cannot answer,
> you must find out for yourself.

In **Section 47**, Whitman makes direct assertions of his principle of self-reliance:

> He that by me spreads a wider breast than my own proves the width of my own,
> He most honors my style who learns under it to destroy the teacher.
> The boy I love, the same becomes a man not through divided power,
> but in his own right, . . .

Whitman recommends that whatever you may be, you should be so by your own choice and because of your own individuality:

> Wicked rather than virtuous out of conformity or fear, . . .

SECTIONS 48-50

At this point in "Sing of Myself," there is a sudden series of restatements of the essential ideas of the poem:

> I have said that the soul is not more than the body,
> And I have said that the body is not more than the soul,
> And nothing, not God, is greater to one than one's self is,
>
> . . . . .
>
> And I say to any man or woman, Let your soul stand cool and
> compos'd before a million universes.
>
> . . . . .
>
> I hear and behold God in every object, yet understand

God not in the least,
Nor do I understand who there can be more wonderful than myself.

. . . . .

And as to you Death, and you bitter hug of mortality, it is idle to try to alarm me.

. . . . .

And as to you Life I reckon you are the leavings of many deaths,
(No doubt I have died myself ten thousand times before.)

. . . . .

There is that in me - I do not know what it is - but I know it is in me.

. . . . .

It is not chaos or death - it is form, union, plan -

it is eternal life - it is Happiness.

SECTION 51-52

The cycle of the poem is approaching completion. The poet, like each component of the universe, has completed a phase of the great evolutionary process.

The past and present wilt -

**I have fill'd them, emptied them,
And proceed to fill my next fold of the future.**

There is a spirit of impatience and of preparation for departure in the poetic voice:

**(Talk honestly, no one else hears you,
and I stay only a minute longer.)
Do I contradict myself?
Very well then I contradict myself,
(I am large, I contain multitudes.)**

In these last three lines, Whitman implies that the greatness and capacity of "self" must be taken on faith, for trivialities are swallowed up in its vastness. He maintains a supreme confidence in the orderly relationship of spirit, matter, and man. His faith sees apparent contradictions less as knotty problems and more as acceptable mysteries or paradoxes within the great order of the universe.

The pace quickens as the poet prepares to hurry off into the progression of evolution and reincarnation. Like the "spotted hawk," he too is "untranslatable." With the appearance of some timeless and primitive figure, he is ready to re-enter the cyclic pattern of nature.

**I sound my barbaric yawp over the roofs of the world.
The last scud of the day holds back for me,**

. . . . .

It coaxes me to the vapor and the dust.

There is no "death" for Whitman, no ultimate "dissolution." He will fuse with the pantheistic "grass," the symbol of eternal and reincarnating life:

> I bequeath myself to the dirt to grow from the grass I love,
> If you want me again look for me under your bootsoles.
>
> . . . . .
>
> Failing to fetch me at first keep encouraged,
> Missing me one place search another,
> I stop somewhere waiting for you.

"Song of Myself" ends with this promise by Whitman of an eternal pattern of reincarnation and immortality, and contentment in it.

SUMMARY AND EVALUATION

"Song of Myself" is the longest poem in *Leaves of Grass*. Its nearly 1,350 lines represent more than half of the 1855 edition. It is far from perfect poetry; if we search for refinement in its overall poetic structure, we will be disappointed. The poem can give the impression of being overextended. A reader desiring surface unity can expect to discover little. Although various portions of it are tightly assembled, the fifty-two sections of different lengths often seem to be ill-matched and in need of consistent and proper transition. The long catalogues, an experiment on Whitman's part, have been criticized for being overpadded, unsorted jumbles, lacking any indispensable components.

As pure poetry, "Song of Myself" is best appreciated in its parts. It has many exciting and poetically sound sections, but the quality is not sustained and the reader is often conscious of being interrupted by passages that seem remarkably unpoetic. Certainly, the poem lacks the ordered development and emotional beauty that we will meet when we examine three of Whitman's best and most famous works: "Out of the Cradle Endlessly Rocking," "When Lilacs Last in the Dooryard Bloom'd," and "Crossing Brooklyn Ferry."

Up to this point, we have looked at the negative side of the poem. The positive side is compelling enough to convince us that "Song of Myself" is an example of great American poetry. The **imagery** is splendid. If Whitman's catalogues do appear overly cluttered on occasion, they are redeemed by their sharply focused series of tiny portraits from nature and every walk of life. We have remarked that charges of carelessness in selecting the items of the catalogues are substantially weakened when we observe Whitman's care in pairing and contrasting the variety of figures he presented. In short, "Song of Myself" contains many beautiful and striking details.

The poem possesses unity, but not in the most traditional sense. We become aware of an abstract unity when we have read it completely and thoroughly. By abstract, we mean that the unity is not found in the technical structure of the poem. However, one aspect of unity is present in Whitman's poetic "direction." Through his mystical experiences, he arrives at an understanding of "self" and its place in a cosmic patterns of life, death, and infinite rebirth. There is a steady movement through a broad variety of experiences, but the direction is always toward the ultimate illumination and understanding that the poet finally achieves. The examination of "self," and the apparently aimless visionary journeys through time and space, are bound together in contributing to the poet's ultimate spiritual awareness. From the "loafe at my ease" of **Section 1**, to the growing insight of "it is true when I guess'd at" in **Section 33**, Whitman passes through visions and impressions that are unclear and mysterious. **Sections 48 through 50** represent a high plateau of enlightenment where the poet ties together what had previously been scattered. If we understand the poem's movement toward an awareness that is clear and satisfying, it does not seem unreasonable that the path leading there would appear cluttered, disjointed, and perhaps even illogical in its progression of ideas.

It will be recalled that in *Inscriptions* we saw the isolated Whitman **themes** introduced. "Starting from Paumanok" brought those ideas together in a single poem and set their development in motion. "Song of Myself" expands them even more. If that development appears unbounded and undisciplined, much of the impression of disorder is lost when we remind ourselves that Whitman is exploring and developing many ideas over the course of his fifty-two "chants." We cannot, therefore, look for unity along a single thread of thought.

The individuality that the poet endorses in the poem is practiced in its composition; he allowed no restrictions, technically or topically. Whitman's novel **syntax** and the variety of his vocabulary offer an exciting experience in language. "Song of Myself" can charge the reader's emotions, particularly when it is read aloud, allowing Whitman's fondness for the oratorical style to be best displayed. Regardless of the many sound criticisms that point up the poem's failings, it remains a compelling piece of American literature.

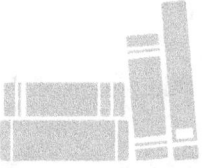

CHILDREN OF ADAM

BACKGROUND

The third edition of *Leaves of Grass*, printed in 1860, contained a section entitled *Enfans d' Adam* (*Children of Adam*). It was composed of fifteen poems, twelve of which were then published for the first time. It was not until the 1867 edition of the book that the section was called *Children of Adam*, a title which was retained throughout subsequent editions. At this time, the entire group was moved, from the center of the book, nearer the beginning, directly after "Song of Myself." *Children of Adam* and the following group, *Calamus*, became the most notorious bodies of verse in *Leaves of Grass*. They prompted a great variety of responses from the public and the critics alike, even resulting in Whitman's dismissal from a minor government post.

Ralph Waldo Emerson was the first American man of letters to acknowledge openly the merit of Leaves following its 1855 publication. However, perhaps anticipating the indignant reaction that the *Enfans d' Adam* group would cause, or considering the group to be too indelicate, he advised Whitman not to include the poems. Whitman was immovable. The poems were "More precious than gold . . ." to him, and he would not suppress them. Much of the public reaction was predictable; even Henry David Thoreau, himself a friend and admirer of

Whitman, observed that the voice of the poems was like that of the "beasts."

Charges of indecency did not take into account Whitman's belief in the basic purity and integrity of all things in nature. While the poems clash sharply with conventional social attitudes regarding male and female relationships, they are totally compatible with the poet's belief in the wholesomeness of the human body in its identity with the soul, and his unwillingness to accept traditional ideas of good and evil. At the heart of the *Children of Adam* poems is the **theme** of the great cycle of human reproduction, moved forward infinitely by the expression of sexual love. They express love between male and female, but should not be considered as love poems in the traditional sense.

"TO THE GARDEN THE WORLD"

With this poem, the group commences in an outburst of Whitman's belief in the cyclic pattern of human reproduction:

> To the garden the world anew ascending,
> Potent mates, daughters, sons, preluding,
> The love, the life of their bodies, meaning and being,
> Curious here behold my resurrection after slumber,
> The revolving cycles in their wide sweep having brought me again,
> Amorous, mature, all beautiful to me, all wonderous,
> . . .

The poet has come to his present existence like a new Adam to the Old Testament Garden of Eden. He is a product and a part of all males and females of the past and the result of the physical union of their love. We can see here another aspect of

Whitman's idea of an infinite line of life and nature along which man appears and reappears in life cycles. In this instance, the focus is upon human procreation, human renewal through the act of sexual union.

Linked to Adam by endless generations, the poet stands in the present with his own Eve, the symbol of the necessary mate. Unlike the first Eve, Whitman's Eve enjoys total equality with the male, a notion proper to Whitman's plan for celebrating the "female equal with the male."

> **By my side or back of me Eve following,**
> **Or in front, and I following her just the same.**

The cycle is renewed and will be renewed as with the first man and woman; new but unchanged, it moves ahead in a pattern of sexual love and reproduction.

"FROM PENT-UP ACHING RIVERS"

After the majestic Biblical texture of the opening poem, Whitman asserts his desire and need to write of sexual love:

> **From pent-up aching rivers,**
> **From that of myself without which I were nothing,**
> **From what I am determin'd to make illustrious, even**
> **if I stand sole among men, . . .**

These lines are like a personal declaration when we read them. They seem to be a firm and direct reply to Emerson's objections in 1860. The poet is

> **Singing the song of procreation,**

> Singing the need of superb children and therein superb grown people, . . .

These ideas share in the broad philosophic core of *Leaves of Grass*. The poet abandons himself to the mysterious force of sexual passions and their gratification:

> From the hungry gnaw that eats me night and day,
>
> . . . . .
>
> The mystic deliria, the madness amorous, the utter abandonment,
>
> . . . . .
>
> Two hawks in the air, two fishes swimming in the sea not more lawless than we;) . . .

The poet's eyes always seem to be on the endless family of man, stretching ahead through eternity and enduring through the sexual reproductive act - an act that is sacred, for it reproduces man, who is sublime to Whitman.

> . . . I emerging flitting out,
> Celebrate you act divine and you
> children prepared for,
> And you stalwart loins.

"I SING THE BODY ELECTRIC"

This, the longest poem in the Adam group, was extensively revised after its appearance in the first edition. In its final form, the poem represents the philosophic voice of the poet rather than an intense personal outburst of sexual expression. We can see in it the reappearance of familiar Whitman attitudes - the celebration of the body and the identity of body with soul.

> **I sing the body electric,**
>
> **. . . . .**
>
> **And if the body does not do fully as much as the soul?**
> **And if the body were not the soul, what is the soul?**
> **The love of the body of man or woman balks account,**
> **the body itself balks account,**
> **That of the male is perfect, and that of the female is perfect.**

The poems contains a lengthy catalogue in which bodily contour and movement dazzle the poet. In a typical Whitman panoramic vision, clusters of people appear "in all their performances."

> **But the expression of a well-made man appears**
> **not only in his face,**
>
> **. . . . .**
>
> **It is in his walk, the carriage of his neck,**
> **the flex of his waist and knees,**
> **dress does not hide him,**
>
> **. . . . .**
>
> **The sprawl and fullness of babes,**
> **the bosoms and heads of women,**

. . . . .

> The bending forward and backward of rowers in rowboats,
> the horseman in his saddle, . . .

In the third section of the poem, we are reminded of the group's title, *Children of Adam*, as Whitman suddenly thrusts before us the figure of a noble and aged native American.

> I knew a man, a common farmer,
> the father of five sons,
> And in them the fathers of five sons,
> and in them the fathers of sons. . . .

Is the image of father Adam and Adam's children and their children's children - generation after generation repeated over and over again in a great plan of procreation. The aged man is majestic in appearance, "of wonderful vigor, calmness, [and] beauty of person." He is tall, erect and godlike in the eyes of the poet, one of "the breed of fullsized men . . . unconquerable and simple" that Whitman spoke of in the preface to the first edition of *Leaves of Grass*. As "a common farmer," he is a splendid and proud member of Whitman's "aristocracy" of the American man.

> He was six feet tall, he was over eighty years old,
> his sons were massive, clean, bearded,
> tan-faced, handsome,
> They and his daughters loved him,
> all who saw him loved him, . . .

The tone and movement of the lines are almost Biblical, and the figure is much like the wise head of a tribe or nation. There is an aura of distant time and legendary perfection about the man, but Whitman makes the picture immediate, mixing that timelessness with the aged man's physical magnetism:

> **You would wish long and long to be with him,**
> **you would wish to sit by him in the boat**
> **that you and he might touch each other.**

This "common farmer" is the vigorous representation of the ideal male for Whitman. He has a natural and wholesome simplicity. Venerable and ageless, he radiates a robust masculinity.

> **He drank water only, the blood show'd like scarlet**
> **through the clear-brown skin of his face, . . .**

In his personal life, Whitman was acutely conscious of the sense of touch, a characteristic that is evident in many of the sensual passages of his poetry. This sensitivity is obvious in **Section 4** of "I Sing the Body Electric":

> **To pass among them or touch any one, or rest my arm**
> **ever so lightly round his or her neck**
> **for a moment, what is this then?**
> **I do not ask any more delight, I swim in it as in a sea.**

In **Section 5**, Whitman celebrates the female body and its high purpose in the infinite cycle of human reproduction:

> **This is the female form,**
> **A divine nimbus exhales from it from**
> **head to foot,**
> **It attracts with fierce undeniable attraction,**
>
> **. . . . .**

> This the nucleus - after the child is born of woman,
> man is born of woman,
>
> . . . . .
>
> Be not ashamed women, your privilege encloses the rest,
> and is the exit of the rest,
> You are the gates of the body, and you are the gates of the soul.

Whitman's praise of women is no hymn of love to the beauty of womankind. What he honors here is their function of conceiving and giving birth to generations of humanity. The woman is "the exit of the rest," the one from whom the infinite chain of humanity proceeds.

> The female contains all qualities and tempers them,
>
> . . . . .
>
> She is all things duly veil'd,
> she is both passive and active,
> She is to conceive daughters as well as sons,
> and sons as well as daughters.

Section 6 of the poem honors the male body, equally with the female's and the place of each in the great cosmic order that Whitman visualizes:

> The male is not less the soul nor more,
> he too is in his place,
> The man's body is sacred and the woman's body is sacred,

. . . . .

**Each has his or her place in the procession.
(All is a procession,
The universe is a procession with measured and perfect motion.)**

In Whitman's "Universe" of "measured and perfect motion," all people, regardless of who they are - "the meanest one of the laborers' gang" or "the dull-faced immigrants" - possess bodies that have beauty and significance in the evolutionary order and development of the universe.

**Do you think matter has cohered together from its diffuse float, and the soil is on the surface, and water runs and vegetation sprouts,
For you only, and not for him or her?**

In the slave market, the poet saw

A man's body at auction, ...

That body or anybody is beyond any price whatsoever:

Gentlemen look on this wonder, ...

It is the achievement of endless human cycles; it defies market value:

**Whatever the bids of the bidders they
cannot be high enough for it,
For it the globe lay preparing quintillions of years without one animal or plant,
For it the revolving cycles truly and steadily roll'd.**

The human body holds the potential of the race, the promise of the future, and the seed of life immortal.

> This is not only one man, this the father of those who shall be fathers in their turns,
>
> .....
>
> How do you know who shall come from the offspring through the centuries?
> (Who might you find you have come from yourself, if you could trace back through the centuries?)

The female slave at auction inspires the poet in the same fashion; he sees in her not merely the individual, but the reservoir of peoples.

> She too is not only herself,
> she is the teeming mother of mothers,
> She is the bearer of them that shall grow and be mates to the mothers.
>
> .....
>
> If anything is sacred the human body is sacred,...

In **Section 9**, the final section of the poem, Whitman constructs a detailed catalogue of the parts, organs and functions of the body; there is little that he omits. The catalogue, which was added to the 1856 edition, is little more than a mechanical recitation and has little if any poetic merit.

Toward the very end of "I Sing the Body Electric," Whitman relieves the tedium of his catalogue with a few satisfying images that rise to a successful poetic emotion:

> The circling rivers the breath,
> and breathing it in and out,
>
> . . . . .
>
> The exquisite realization of health;
> O I say these are not the parts and poems of the
> body only, but of the soul,
> Oh I say now these are the soul!

"A WOMAN WAITS FOR ME"

For Whitman, the sexual activity of the body and its parts represents a sacred and spiritual act embracing the fullness of life itself. In "A Woman Waits for Me," Whitman says this precisely:

> Sex contains all, bodies, souls,
> Meanings, proofs, purities, delicacies,
> results, promulgations,
>
> . . . . .
>
> All hopes, benefactions, bestowals,
> all the passions, loves, beauties,
> delights of the earth,
>
> . . . . .

These are contain'd in sex as parts of itself
and justifications of itself.

Because sexual activity is a human function that generates the future of nations and races, Whitman allows for no sense of shame whatsoever; the essential purity of sex cannot be questioned by him.

**Without shame the man I like knows and avows
the deliciousness of his sex,
Without shame the woman I like knows and avows hers.**

The poet bellows loudly as the spokesman and ideal of the virile male in whom lies the seed of future people. The poet's persona speaks in a hearty boastfulness, with a commanding force that cannot be denied:

**I see that they are worthy of me,
I will be the robust husband of those women.**

. . . . .

**Envelop'd in you sleep greater heroes and bards,
They refuse to wake at the touch of any man but me.**

. . . . .

**I shall demand perfect men and women
out of my love-spendings, . . .**

"SPONTANEOUS ME"

Whitman's attitude toward love and sex appears to be essentially unchanged from Biblical ideas of the uncontaminated natural purity of Adam and Eve before their temptation and fall from God's favor. The poet sees the physical relationship of man and woman set in a type of neo-Eden, devoid of social taboos and frustrations. Whitman's man and woman are emancipated - free to receive guiltless pleasure and gratification both from each other and from the thought of their high purpose as members and part creators of the infinite human chain. Physical love is unconfined and natural for the poet, representing a wholesome and basic human force. In "Spontaneous Me," the atmosphere is one of a timeless Eden, a sensual and lush paradise. It is a poem whose very title suggests that to restrain the natural drives in man is to restrain nature itself.

> **Spontaneous me, Nature,**
>
> .....
>
> **Earth of chaste love, life that is only life after love,**
> **The body of my love, the body of the woman I love,**
> **the body of the man, the body of the earth,**
> **Soft forenoon airs that blow from the south-west,**
> **The hairy wild-bee that murmers and hankers up**
> **and down, . . .**
>
> .....
>
> **The wet woods through the early hours,**
>
> .....

> The oath of procreation I have sworn,
> my Adamic and fresh daughters, . . .

"ONE HOUR TO MADNESS AND JOY"

This poem reveals the poet in a high pitch of passionate yearning.

> One hour to madness and joy. O furious! O confine me not!
>
> . . . . .
>
> O to drink the mystic deliria deeper than any other man!
>
> . . . . .
>
> O to return to Paradise! O bashful and feminine!

The poet wishes to abandon himself to wild, uncontrolled love-making. The persistent repetition of "O" and "To" at the beginning of lines builds a powerful erotic tension in the poetry. This is not the measured philosophic movement of "I Sing the Body Electric" or the majesty of the timeless Adam figure reincarnated as the noble "common farmer"; this is the insistent voice of passion defying society in its desire for freedom and physical gratification.

> O to be yielded to you whoever you are,
> and you to be yielded to me in
> defiance of the world!
>
> . . . . .

> To be absolv'd from previous ties and conventions,
> I from mine and you from yours!
>
> . . . . .
>
> To escape utterly from others' anchors and holds!
> To drive free! to love free! to dash reckless and dangerous!
>
> . . . . .
>
> To feed the remainder of life with one hour
> of fulness and freedom!
> With one brief hour of madness and joy.

It is necessary to maintain an awareness of Whitman's unconcern for taboos and his coloring of sex with overtones of its social potential and worthy place in a cyclic order of life and the universe. What seems to be social defiance in Whitman is to him only a perfect expression of uninhibited love.

"WE TWO, HOW LONG WE WERE FOOL'D"

The spirit of the poem is that of emancipation from sexual conventions after a long period of socially acceptable conduct.

> Now transmuted, we swiftly escape as Nature escapes.
>
> . . . . .
>
> We browse, we are two among the wild herds spontaneous as any,

. . . . .

The release from restraint makes the physical love between the male and female as free and natural as the existence of the plants, trees, and wildlife of the forest. It will be recalled that Thoreau did not hear in these poems the sublime "amativeness," as Whitman called it, between male and female; instead, he remarked that he heard the sounds of "beasts." In "Song of Myself," the animals possessed a natural simplicity and wholesome condition that the poet attained only after a mystical struggle and purification. For Whitman, "beasts" are not contemptible, but possess a natural and enviable virtue. In many ways, he sees them as models for mankind. In Whitman's philosophy, whatever is natural cannot be wrong.

This poem exposes once again Whitman's faith in reincarnation and an evolutionary cycle in life and the universe. Behind the comparison to things wild and free is the idea that we have been, or could become, any of these many parts of nature:

**We are Nature, long have we been absent,
but now we return,
We become plants, trunks, foliage, roots, bark,**

. . . . .

We are two fishes swimming in the sea together,

. . . . .

**We have circled and circled till we have arrived home again,
we two, . . .**

In the cycles of reincarnation in Whitman's great cosmic order, the lovers, male and female, have come at last to a sexual freedom as uncomplicated and unrestricted as nature itself. It is not unnatural to act so spontaneously; as components of nature, they take to that freedom characteristically.

For Whitman, the sensation of sexual freedom seems not unlike that if sudden spiritual insight. For him, sexual purity is highly disposed to physical release rather than rigid control; with it goes the belief that social taboos are the real immoralities, since they are contrary to nature.

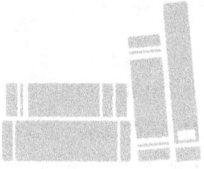

TWO FINAL POEMS

....

"Facing West from California's Shores" directs Whitman's attention toward the Orient, which he believed to be the location of the origin of life.

> **Facing west from California's shores,**
> **Inquiring, tireless, seeking what is yet unfound,**
> **I, a child, very old, over waves, towards the house of maternity, the land of migrations, look afar, . . .**

The persistent Whitman notion of evolving life cycles, moving and returning through forms of existence, appears again in this poem:

> **Long have I wander'd since,**
> **round the earth having wander'd,**
> **Now I face home again,**
> **very pleas'd and joyous, . . .**

In the final poem of the group, "As Adam Early in the Morning," the organic cycle of life appears in the vivid figure of Adam "Walking forth . . . refresh'd" in the Garden of Eden. There is a reminder here of the strong sexual significance for Whitman in the sense of touch. The poet invites us to be unafraid in the natural expression of physical love:

As Adam early in the morning,
Walking forth from the bower refresh'd with sleep,
Behold me where I pass, hear my voice, approach,
Touch me, touch the palm of your hand to my body as I pass,
Be not afraid of my body.

SUMMARY

The poems of the *Children of Adam* group celebrate sexual love between male and female, but are not actually love poems. Whitman discovers in the physical relationship between man and woman an act capable of producing future generations of beautiful and intelligent people. Love-making ("amativeness") should be a free and natural function. Social taboos on sex have no place in Whitman's view, for he believes sex to be pure and wholesome. The poet's "song of procreation" links male and female sexual love to his vision of a great American nation of the future. He also considers it a functional part of the cyclic pattern in the universe.

The *Children of Adam* group maintains no single consistent sexual theme. The idea of human reproduction, while foremost, is often interrupted in its movement by feverish erotic outbursts. A philosophical tone in one poem ("I Sing the Body Electric") is offset by the passionate vigor of another ("One Hour to Madness and Joy"). Whitman's philosophic reflections at one moment are often overtaken by a real and consuming lustiness in the next, causing an unevenness in transition from one poem to another. There are some bright poetic moments as well as some tedious mechanical exercises, but the poetic artistry has caused less controversy than the question of taste in the subject matter. Emerson opposed the inclusion of the group as a whole. Thoreau thought it animalistic, and the discovery of Whitman as the author contributed to his dismissal from a minor government post.

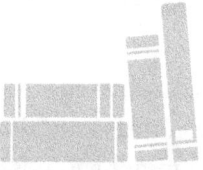

CALAMUS

BACKGROUND

The name *Calamus* appeared at the head of a group of forty-five poems in the 1860 edition of *Leaves of Grass*. They were poems that expressed "cohesiveness," as Whitman called it: the strong love of one man for another, a counterbalancing emotion to the "amativeness," or love between male and female, in the *Children of Adam*. This expression of male, or homosexual, love is made with abundant tenderness and calmness rather than with the stormy passion and boastfulness of the *Children of Adam*. While both groups can be recognized as sex poems, it is more accurate to consider the *Calamus* section as the actual love poetry in the book - regardless of the unorthodox character of that love. There is much of Whitman's own personality and nature in these poems, for it is a fact that he was abnormally attracted to other men. Whatever the irregularities of his personality were, we must recall the poet's rejection of traditional notions of evil and immorality. Male love was, therefore, as legitimate and as pure for Whitman as male-female love. In addition, this male "cohesiveness" was a creative relationship for the poet, because he saw in it a bond of masculine comradeship reaching across the nation.

The title that Whitman gave to these poems is significant to our understanding of the ideas contained in the group. In 1867, Whitman wrote to the eminent English critic, William Michael Rossetti, regarding "a volume of selections from my *Leaves*" to be published in England. Concerning the title of the *Calamus* group, Whitman observed that

> Calamus is a common word here. It is a very large & aromatic grass, or rush, growing about waterponds in the valleys ... The ... sense of the term, as used in my book, arises probably from the actual

> Calamus presenting the biggest & hardiest kind of spears of grass - and their fresh, aquatic, pungent bouquet.

Whitman's association of "biggest and hardiest" with male love poems indicates that the poet looked upon the emotions they contained not as something weak or puny but as wholly compatible with an image of male strength and character.

The poet's sincerity found little sympathy with public reaction. Moreover, it was the discovery of Whitman as the author of the *Calamus* poems along with the *Children of Adam* group, that prompted the Secretary of the interior, James Harlan, to dismiss Whitman from his position as a government clerk in June of 1865. This was done because of the "outrageous" nature of the writing.

"IN PATHS UNTRODDEN"

Whitman begins the section with the lyrical poem "In Paths Untrodden." This poem performs the same function as did "To the Garden the World" at the head of the *Children of Adam* group.

Both establish the basic **themes** of their respective sections, as the various poems of *Inscriptions* did for the book as a whole. In the *Children of Adam* poems, Whitman sounded his joyous enthusiasm for a liberated and natural love between man and woman, a love that contained uninhibited pleasure for its own sake as well as for a purposeful and creative act.

The loud, self-confident voice of the *Adam* poems gives way in the *Calamus* group to a nearly whispered hesitancy. Male and female passions were not emotional forces reserved for the very few. They were universal human characteristics, and so the poet's confident voice reflected common urges, whether or not such a bold presentation was socially acceptable. *Calamus*, however, stands as the outpouring of rarer and traditionally abnormal emotions. Therefore, the feeling of secret sharing and seclusion that the group betrays is altogether understandable.

In paths untrodden,

. . . . .

Escaped from the life that exhibits itself,
From all the standards hitherto publish'd,
from the pleasures, profits, conformities,
Which too long I was offering to feed my soul, . . .

In the seclusion of nature, the poet discovers the calamus reed:

In the growth by margins of water-ponds,

. . . . .

Here by myself away from the clank of the world,

Tallying and talk'd to here by tongues aromatic, . . .

The communion between the poet and the blades of calamus gives a strong sensual impression. Here, in private, he is free to "respond" to those secret urges that he must stifle in society:

**No longer abash'd, (for in this secluded spot I can respond
as I would not dare elsewhere,)
Resolv'd to sing no songs to-day but those of manly attachment,**

. . . . .

**I proceed for all who are or have been young men,
To tell the secret of my nights and days,
To celebrate the need of comrades.**

In the poet's "need of comrades" there is the undeniable force of the homosexual love of male for male. However, in Whitman's term, "manly love," there is also a strong cry for those unaltering male friendships whose bonds of comradeship are merely powerfully fraternal. In addition, the reader must keep before him an awareness of that intense love and sense of adoring kinship for all humanity that is so peculiarly Whitman's.

"SCENTED HERBAGE OF MY BREAST"

One of the most curious poems of the *Calamus* section is "Scented Herbage of My Breast." The mystical and puzzling nature of the poem arises from the strange symbol of "Scented herbage" together with a meditation on love and death. The tone of the poem, like that of the group as a whole, is personal; the reader is half conscious of overhearing Whitman in the privacy of the confessional. Whitman's "barbaric yawp" is silent here; his boastful vigor has slackened to a subdued, almost hesitant, expression.

Whitman thinks of his poems as "Leaves," so personal an expression, and so entrusted with his intimate thoughts and emotions, that they are seen as parts of an organic growth, a "Scented herbage," a rooted cluster springing from the most private and secret part of his being. The poems - or "Leaves" - are

> **Tomb-leaves, body-leaves growing up above me above death,**
>
> **. . . . .**
>
> **O I do not know whether many passing by will discover you**
> **or inhale your faint odor, but I believe a few will;**
> **O slender leaves! O blossoms of my blood! I permit you**
> **to tell in your own way of the heart that is under you,**
> **. . .**

Whitman looks to his poems to be "Perennial," to endure beyond the poet himself and be received by at least a small group - those "few" that would discover and savor his verse.

The poet then contemplates death and love. "(What indeed is finally beautiful except death and love?)" We have seen that the notion of death in Whitman's poetry represents no finality for life. On the contrary, death leads to rebirth in an unending cycle. Therefore, the prospect of death is not mournful or gloomy for him. Its quiet beauty and peace seem not at all unwelcome to his vision of manly love.

> **For how calm, how solemn it grows to ascend**
> **to the atmosphere of lovers,**
> **Death or life I am then indifferent,**
> **my soul declines to prefer,**
> **(I am not sure but the high soul of lovers welcomes death most,) . . .**

The same promise of life that Whitman's "death" holds is discovered in the very nature of his poems - the "Leaves." The poet calls upon his poetry to liberate the long-secreted emotions of manly love that have been concealed within him.

> **Spring away from the conceal'd heart there!**
> **Do not fold yourself so in your pink-tinged roots timid leaves!**
> **Do not remain down there so ashamed, herbage of my breast!**
> **Come I am determin'd to unbare this broad breast of mine,**
> **I have long enough stifled and choked; . . .**

With a feeling of emancipated manly love that parallels the liberated male-female love in the *Children of Adam* group, the poet's voice grows bolder:

> **I will sound myself and comrades only,**
> **I will never again utter a call only their call,**
> **I will raise with it immortal reverberations through the States,**
> **I will give an example to lovers to take permanent shape**

and will through the States, . . .

The poet seems to come alive from the heavy, somber **imagery** of "Scented herbage," "Tomb-leaves," and "winter" by being stimulated by the thought of death:

Through me shall the words be said to make death exhilarating.

Death, with a long literary tradition as the enemy of love, finds no such mismatch in Whitman. There exists a natural compatibility between the two ideas that prompts the poet to say:

**Give me your tone therefore O death,
that I may accord with it,
Give me yourself, for I see that you belong to me
now above all, and are folded inseparably together,
you love and death are, . . .**

Whitman concludes that love and death are the true significances behind life and reality.

**For now it is convey'd to me that you are
the purports essential,
That you hide in these shifting forms of life,
for reasons, and that they are mainly for you,
That you beyond them come forth to remain,
the real reality
That behind the mask of materials you patiently wait,
no matter how long, . . .**

We have seen that love is a "kelson" of the universe for Whitman, and that death is part of the infinite pattern of reincarnation. In the final line of the poem, both of these ideas are projected prophetically with an unfamiliar reserve:

But you will last very long.

This is unusual understatement for Whitman, but an implication of the poet's strong faith in the eternal nature of love and death is evident. This poem seems to invade Whitman's own privacy; its initial somber beauty appears to unlock a bit of the poet's soul. Whitman finds a hopeful prospect in a traditionally somber subject-death-and observes that it is spiritually entwined with manly love.

LOVER-PATRIOT-ORATOR

In "Whoever You are Holding me Now in Hand," there is a cautious and warning invitation to male love:

The way is suspicious, the result uncertain, perhaps destructive,

. . . . .

The whole past theory of your life and all conformity to the lives around you would have to be abandon'd,
. . .

The affectionate "comrade's long dwelling kiss" is received with caution, but much of the unsure manner might have been better expected in the man-woman attachments of the *Adam* poems.

Whitman's enthusiasm for a male and female love that would produce great future generations, "sons and daughters fit for these States," now finds its creative counterpart in "the manly love of comrades." The poet has drawn this *Calamus* love from the private seclusion of his own heart and of the hearts of those "few" who understand and share similar emotions. At this point, he visualizes a utopian society of radiant and matchless "comrades":

> **Come, I will make the continent indissoluble,**
> **I will make the most splendid race the sun ever shown upon,**
> **I will make divine magnetic lands,**
> **With the love of comrades,**
> **With the life-long love of comrades.**
> **"For You O Democracy"**

This patriotic cry is typical of Whitman's ever-widening optimism. He has converted the shy, hesitant "manly attachment" of "In Paths Untrodden" to an enthusiastic vision of socially creative and democratic masculine friendship.

Whitman is less convincing when he chants patriotically of *Calamus* love. It is only when he does not allow "manly love" to attach itself to any social dreams that the poet seems convincing and sincere. The Whitman persona becomes transparent and the poetic voice highly personal when the affection of masculine love, by itself, is felt or contemplated:

> **Not in this beating and pounding at my temples and wrists,**
>
> . . . . .

> Not in the murmurs of my dreams while I sleep,
>
> . . . . .
>
> Not in any or all of them O adhesiveness!
> O pulse of my life!
> Need I that you exist and show yourself any more
> than in these songs.
> "Not Heaving From My Ribb'd Breast Only"

The mere presence of the "comrade" is a great gratification for the poet:

> When he whom I love travels with me or sits a long while
> holding me by the hand,
>
> . . . . .
>
> Then I am charged with untold and untellable wisdom,
> I am silent, I require nothing further,
>
> . . . . .
>
> He ahold of my hand has completely satisfied me.
> "Of the Terrible Doubt of Appearances"

With that strong oratorical flare, he becomes as dramatic as any extravagant **elegy** or **epitaph** verse on a tombstone:

> Recorders ages hence,
>
> . . . . .

> Publish my name and hang up my picture as that
> of the tenderest lover,
> The friend the lover's portrait, of whom his friend
> his lover was fondest,
>
> . . . . .
>
> Who often walk'd lonesome walks thinking
> of his dear friends, his lovers.
> "Recorders Ages Hence"

"WHEN I HEARD AT THE CLOSE OF DAY"

The rhetorical composition of "Recorders Ages Hence" is effective, but cannot equal the beautiful balance of pace and emotion in "When I Heard at the Close of Day." The poem begins in an atmosphere of restrained but persistent unrest:

> When I heard at the close of the day
> how my name had been receiv'd with plaudits in the capitol,
> still it was not a happy night for me that follow'd, . . .

The steady, fluid motion, and the repetition of "When" in the beginning and middle of lines, quicken the pulse and provide the poem with a sense of direction - an upward motion toward an emotionally climactic level. After the poet contemplates the approach of his loving "comrade," he attains a high point of bright emotion:

> And when I thought how my dear friend my lover
> was on his way coming, O then I was happy,
> O then each breath tasted sweeter,

> and all that day my food nourish'd me more,
> and the beautiful day pass'd well, ...

The emotion does not descend rapidly, but instead evens out to quiet satisfaction and comfort in the comrade's presence:

> In the stillness in the autumn moonbeams his face
> was inclined toward me,
> And his arm lay lightly around my breast -
> and that night I was happy.

In this **free verse** poem, Whitman comes closer to a more recognizable poetic structure. He is conscious of a need for poise and balance if the mood is to be adequately sustained, and these he achieves with careful equilibrium in the lines:

> ... when I carous'd ... when ... plans accomplish'd
>
> . . . . .
>
> When I wander'd ... and ... bathed ... and saw ...
>
> . . . . .
>
> ... breath tasted ... food nourish'd ... day pass'd ...

In order to comprehend the beauty of this poem, the reader must not allow Whitman's expression of manly love to cloud his appreciation. If the poem is enjoyed simply as an outpouring of love freed of any biographical or uncomfortable associations, the beauty is abundantly evident. One lover yearning for the return of the other - the meeting at last - the perfect contentment of their bond: the pattern is eternal and the emotion transcends immediate associations.

"I SAW IN LOUISIANA A LIVE OAK GROWING"

This is a very personal poem in which the solitary, manly lover-poet compares himself to an erect and mighty oak. The "oak" is a traditional symbol of strength; Whitman's use of it is in keeping with his ideas of robust male love and the nobility and freedom discovered in nature.

> **I saw in Louisiana a live-oak growing,**
> **All alone stood it and the moss hung down from the branches,**
> **Without any companion it grew there uttering joyous leaves of dark green,**
> **And its look, rude, unbending, lusty, made me think of myself, . . .**

With great majesty, the tree stands independent in its solitude. To Whitman, the tree is "uttering" leaves; and if we see these "joyous" leaves as personal expressions growing out from within, they are not unlike those poems in "Scented Herbage of My Breast," which grew organically from the poet. Before the ageless, tranquil oak, the poet confesses his need for manly companionship; he could never be so complete and independent in the face of such loneliness.

> **But I wonder'd how it could utter joyous leaves standing alone there**
> **without its friend near, for I knew I could not, . . .**

The lone, self-sufficient oak stands in strong contrast to the lonely and dejected poet, who takes away with him a "twig with a certain number of leaves upon it." However, Whitman does not need to be reminded of male companions themselves:

(For I believe lately I think of little else than of them,)
. . .

As a "curious token," the "twig" suggests to the poet the male affection between himself and his absent "dear friend." The mood of loneliness and dependence persists to the end of the poem. The poet dwells upon the proud oak, "solitary ... without a friend a lover near," yet spirited and unbent by loneliness. Whitman's voice seems to grow a bit fainter and his head to bow somewhat, as he acknowledges once again his need for his companions and their affection. To live alone as this isolated tree?

I know very well I could not.

SUMMARY

The *Calamus* section of *Leaves of Grass* is a group of love poems that express male affection, or as Whitman termed it, "athletic love" or "manly attachment." The poems are personal and sensitive but lack the boastful surety of the *Children of Adam* group. However, the hesitancy and the almost embarrassingly revealing attitude of many of them make the reader certain of having heard a private confession of love. The confident bellowing of the *Adam* poems betrays a lack of true personal understanding of the relationship involved. On the other hand, Whitman's moderation and delicate approach to *Calamus* love reveals a person more sensitive to this type of affection. The poet is forced to resort to unnatural and fanciful dramatics to make the emotion of the *Adam* poems bear any mark of authority. *Calamus* love should not be made the overwhelming characteristic in the poet, for we also see in him a capacity for strong friendships and great humanitarianism. However, it is reasonable to conclude that Whitman found himself more at ease in the expression of this type of affection. The poet's voice in *Children of Adam* is more like that of a boastful but inexperienced outsider, while the *Calamus* "comrade" seems no stranger to "manly attachment." Whitman saw both types of love as creative forces, the male-female affection as the generator of a splendid future humanity, and the "athletic love" of *Calamus* as a great force for good, one that in the poet's idealization is capable of shaping America into a "divine magnetic" land, strengthened

By the love of comrades,
By the manly love of comrades.

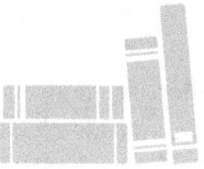

DRUM-TAPS

BACKGROUND

The Civil War had a deep effect on Walt Whitman both as a human being and as a poet. The visible result of the conflict was *Drum-Taps*, a collection of fifty-three poems that appeared in 1865 in the form of a seventy-two-page pamphlet. Later that same year, Whitman reissued the poems with a continuation entitled *Sequel to Drum-Taps*, which included the beautiful **elegy** on Abraham Lincoln, "When Lilacs Last in the Dooryard Bloom'd." Whitman tacked on the *Drum-Taps* poetry to the 1867 edition of *Leaves of Grass*, but it was not until the fifth edition of 1870-71 that the poems were actually incorporated into the main body of his work.

The war began on April 12, 1861, with the attack by the Confederate forces upon Fort Sumter in Charleston, South Carolina. In 1861 and 1862, eleven southern states seceded from the union, and the nation was engaged in the agony of the Civil War. The Whitman family itself was touched by the conflict when the poet's brother George was wounded at the battle of Fredricksberg. In December of 1862, Whitman "went down to the war fields of Virginia" to be near him and to act as an unofficial male nurse in the army hospitals. In a January 1863 letter to Ralph Waldo Emerson, Whitman wrote:

> I go a great deal into the hospitals. Washington is full of them... I desire and intend to write a little book out of this phase of America, her masculine young manhood... prophetic of the future... the imperial blood and rarest marrow of the North... This thing I will record - it belongs to the time, and to all the States - (and perhaps it belongs to me) -

The idea of Americans in battle against Americans shocked Whitman early in the war, and many of the *Drum-Taps* poems were written before his Washington-Virginia trip to visit his wounded brother. Whitman's war experiences, at the hospitals and near the battle front, provided a real and dynamic background for the expression of his democratic ideals and those deep affections which he felt for his fellow man. In *Drum-Taps*, Whitman is artist and reporter, transmitting both what he saw and what he felt; but his sobering experiences did not alter his essential attitudes toward man and existence. The great human conflict actually strengthened his faith in man. It moved his "manly" love into the open, where it appeared as a healthier fraternal and even fatherly affection for the troops about him. His visions of a splendid democracy were sound ones, and the trial and survival of the nation's democratic ideals were a justification of his personal convictions. If he ever doubted the merits of his faith in man and country, the war experiences had reassured him. The Civil War appears to have brought Whitman to a fresh reappraisal of his work. A January 1865 letter from Whitman to William O'Connor reveals the artistic consciousness and sense of fulfillment with which the poet regarded *Drum-Taps*:

> It is in my opinion superior to *Leaves of Grass* - certainly more perfect as a work of art, being adjusted in all its proportions... But I am perhaps mainly satisfied with *Drum-Taps* because it delivers

my ambitions of the task that has haunted me . . . *Drum-Taps* has none of the perturbations of *Leaves of Grass* . . . but there are a few things I shall carefully eliminate in the next issue, & a few more I shall considerably change . . . I have in it only succeeded to my satisfaction in removing all superfluity from it, verbal superfluity I mean. I delight to make a poem where I feel clear that not a word but is indispensable part thereof & of my meaning.

"When Lilacs Last in the Dooryard Bloom'd," printed in *Sequel to Drum-Taps*, represents a bright moment in American poetry; however, taken together, the *Drum-Taps* poems do not appear to be as overshadowing of his other work as Whitman believed. Nevertheless, they do possess greater unity than his output prior to the war.

"FIRST O SONGS FOR A PRELUDE"

This was the first poem in the final arrangement of *Drum-Taps*. Its hushed, almost whispered, first lines are the calm, thoughtful beginning of a narrative of war and patriotic spirit:

> First O songs for a prelude,
> Lightly strike on the stretch'd tympanum pride and joy in my city,
> How she led the rest to arms, how she gave the clue,
>
> . . . . .
>
> How Manhattan drum-taps led.

The poem gathers momentum; in an expectant tempo, Whitman presents a catalogue of people who are equal to the task of preparing for war:

> At dead of night, at news from the south,
>
> . . . . .
>
> To the drum-taps prompt,
> The young men falling in and arming,
>
> . . . . .
>
> The lawyer leaving his office and arming,
> the judge leaving the court,
>
> . . . . .
>
> Squads gather everywhere by common consent and arm,
> The new recruits, even boys, the old men show them how to wear their accoutrements,
> they buckle the straps carefully, . . .

This first poem in *Drum-Taps* contains "The unpent enthusiasm" of the people; Whitman's voice, excited and expectant, rises over the bustle of preparation:

> The blood of the city up-arm'd! arm'd! the cry everywhere, . . .

The city and its people are ready for war; and with them, the poet faces it confidently. It is an example of Whitman's enduring faith in his country and his fellow citizens.

> War! an arm'd race is advancing!
> the welcome for battle, no turning away;
> War! be it weeks, months, or years,
> an arm'd race is advancing to welcome it.

Whitman places exacting demands upon his poems for the struggle at hand. They must have the character and strength of those men and events of which he writes. In "Eighteen Sixty-One," his cry is an explicit one:

> Arm'd year - year of the struggle,
> No dainty rhymes or sentimental love verses
> for you this terrible year,
> Not you as some pale poetling seated at a desk
> lisping cadenzas piano, . . .

"BEAT! BEAT! DRUMS!"

The determined tone of the poetry continues. In "Beat! Beat! Drums!", the call to arms in Whitman's voice cannot be denied; the poem's steady, unrelenting cadence has a sweeping force that pulls all toward the immediate conflict:

> Beat! beat! drums! - blow! bugles! blow!
> Through the windows - through doors -
> burst like a ruthless force, . . .

The movement of the poem is regular and measured. The form is uncomplicated with its three verses, all introduced by the same line, and each with seven lines that are mostly uniform. The even structure of the poem reflects a demand in the poet's voice for uniformity of response from those he addresses. It is not a time for experimentation or individuality, but one of common cause and ordered ranks. The sense of stability contained in a more conventional poetic form seems best to accommodate Whitman's cry for unity in the common cause. There is no welcome for sentiment in the beat of the drums; the anguish of loved ones cannot soften this mighty and clear call:

> **Mind not the old man beseeching the young man,**
> **Let not the child's voice be heard,**
> **nor the mother's entreaties, . . .**

Shrill bugles stir men's blood, and Whitman's constant "drums" measure out a strange and somber appeal:

> **So strong you thump O terrible drums - so loud you bugles blow.**

"THE CENTENARIAN'S STORY"

Whitman's national muster call is now nearly done. His "sword-shaped pennant for war," his "wind piping the pipe of death," and his prodding of "Democracy" to "strike vengeful stroke!", have come through the heated flurries of patriotic reaction. For a moment there is quiet and a mood of timelessness in the poetry. "The Centenarian's Story" provides a brief interlude that halts the poet and the reader on the way to the violent realities of war. In Washington Park, Brooklyn, Whitman converses with an aged veteran of the Revolutionary War as they watch Union troops drilling below them. History reaches forward to touch Whitman, as the poet assists the old soldier:

> **Give me your hand old Revolutionary,**
>
> . . . . .

> Not for nothing have I brought you hither -
> we must remain.
> You to speak in your turn, and I to listen and tell, . . .

The old veteran is moved by the sight to tell the poet of the conflict once fought in Brooklyn in colonial days:

> I tell not the whole story of the battle,
> But one brigade early in the afternoon order'd forward
> to engage the red-coats,
>
> . . . . .
>
> And how long and well it stood confronting death.

The poet feels the presence of the American past, much as he did in "Song of Myself," and persists in his role of spokesman and poet-prophet.

> Enough, the Centenarian's story ends,
> The two, the past and present, have interchanged,
> I myself as connector, as chansonnier of a great future,
> am now speaking.

"CAVALRY CROSSING A FORD"

Whitman's poetic eye is much like that of an artist. He can capture the rare and fleeting image in a few careful strokes. Nowhere is this better illustrated than in "Cavalry Crossing a Ford," a well-made example of picture-poetry. A long line of cavalry is seen moving across a stream - a fleeting, unimportant incident in the Civil War, but caught and held in Whitman's verse. The poet mixes in the proper appeal to both sight and hearing, and the observer is conscious of bright colors and significant sounds:

> **A line in long array where they wind betwixt green islands,**
> **They take a serpentine course, their arms flash in the sun - hark to the musical clank,**
> **Behold the silvery river, in it the splashing horses loitering stop to drink, . . .**

We watch with Whitman as the horsemen pass from shore to shore. For a moment the reader pauses with the "brown-faced" troopers, several of whom are "negligent" and "rest on their saddles." The column moves on; and from individual details, we return to a collective impression of the whole body of mounted men:

> **. . . while,**
> **Scarlet and blue and snowy white,**
> **The guidon flags flutter gayly in the wind, . . .**

The poem is an outstanding example of Whitman's powers of observation at their very best, and convincing evidence of the vigor and bright **imagery** that the Civil War brought to his poetry

"BY THE BIVOUAC'S FITFUL FLAME"

In "Cavalry Crossing a Ford," Whitman observed the movement of soldiers from a distance. In two other brief poems, "Bivouac on a Mountain Side" and "An Army Corps on the March," the poet maintains the same attitude - that of the uninvolved witness.

From the feverish preparations in "First O Songs for a Prelude," the poet has come to the edge of the conflict, to the places where cavalry columns follow a "serpentine course" and where

> The numerous camp-fires scatter'd near and far,
> some away up on the mountain,
> The shadowy forms of men and horses, looming,
> large-sized, flickering. . . .
> "Bivouac on a Mountain Side"

He is aware of vague shapes; he sees the bustle and hears sounds of activity from the distant conflict:

> With its cloud of skirmishers in advance,
> With now the sound of a single shot
> snapping like a whip,
> and now an irregular volley, . . .
> "An Army Corps on the March"

These are still the observations of the reporter or the sketching artist. They reflect the man who is not wholly involved, who as yet shares neither the pangs of fear and homesickness of the young recruit nor the resignation of the stoic veteran.

"By the Bivouac's Fitful Flame" is a poem in which Whitman becomes more of a participant in the war scenes and less an observer. His voice and recollections more closely resemble those of the individual, the foot soldier, suddenly thrust into a new and unfamiliar situation. Whitman dwells upon those thoughts usually reserved for that quiet period of preparation before great and dangerous events. Like the "fitful" flame of the campfire, his thoughts are also restless, finding their way back to "home and the past" and to "those that are far away." As all soldiers must do, he thinks of "life and death." It is appropriate for the solemn mood.

This poem provides a good and necessary contrast to the spirited enthusiasm of the first poems of *Drum-Taps* and to those poems that capture so vividly, yet objectively, the colorful scenes of troops and equipment. In the almost unreal world of "dim outline" and an "occasional figure moving" like some "phantom," Whitman turns from the color and romantic excitement of war to permit his thoughts to wander where they may:

> **While wind in procession thoughts,**
> **O tender and wondrous thoughts,**
>
> **. . . . .**
>
> **A solemn and slow procession there as I sit on the ground,**
> **By the bivouac's fitful flame.**

"COME UP FROM THE FIELDS FATHER"

In March of 1864, Whitman wrote to his mother from Washington. The letter shows much of the same tender compassion that flows through many of the *Drum-Taps* poems and exemplifies Whitman's ability to share in a very personal way the wartime sorrows of others:

> **I came up to the nearest hospital & helped - Mother, it was a dreadful night ... One poor boy ... he seemed to me quite young, he was quite small . . . they set down the stretcher & examined him, & the poor boy was dead ... Mother, it is enough to rack one's heart,**

such things - poor poor child, for he appeared as though he could be but 18 - Mother, when I see the common soldiers, and what they go through, . . . & then the agony I see every day, I get almost frightened at the world -

The voice in the letter feels a personal loss and speaks with the tenderness of a loving parent. "Come up From the Fields Father" contains this same Whitman characteristic - that of reaching beyond humanitarianism to a nearly perfect identification with the sorrow and loss of others. We know that the Civil War touched the poet in a great and enduring way. More than the average sensitive person, he felt anguish close to that of the soldiers and their grieving families. In Whitman's letter, he seems able to speak with feminine, even motherly, emotions. With the same tenderness, he can write of an Ohio farm mother's anxiety and affliction as if he had personally experienced them:

**Come up from the fields father,
here's a letter from our Pete,
And come to the front door mother,
here's a letter from thy dear son.**

. . . . .

**Fast as she can she hurries, something ominous,
her steps trembling,
She does not tarry to smooth her hair nor adjust her cap.**

. . . . .

Open the envelope quickly,

. . . . .

Alas poor boy, he will never be better,
(nor may-be needs to be better,
that brave and simple soul,) . . .

How like Walt Whitman's own gentle and sensitive letter to his mother is the poet's voice in describing the grief of the dead soldier's mother!

By day her meals untouch'd, then at night fitfully sleeping,
often waking,
In the midnight waking, weeping, longing with one deep longing,
O that she might withdraw unnoticed, silent from life escape and withdraw,
To follow, to seek, to be with her dear dead son.

Actually, the poem's title represents artful misdirection. The father is only a background figure - it is the mother who contributes the emotional weight. The seventeenth century English poet John Milton observed that "They also serve who only stand and wait." It is this same eloquent message that Whitman expresses in "Come up from the Fields Father": war brings as great - perhaps even a greater - a measure of pain and suffering to those at home as it does to those on the battlefield.

"VIGIL STRANGE I KEPT ON THE FIELD ONE NIGHT"

Whitman's experiences in tending the wounded in Union hospitals, while poetically stimulating, were certainly painful for the poet. His sensitive nature ached at the thought of the suffering and the great masses of the scattered and half-buried dead, or as he called them, "the varieties of the strayed dead." In *Specimen Days*, Whitman offers some recollections written later in his life from wartime notes; he returns to painful memories of the "dead of this war":

> ... the dead, the dead, the dead - our dead - or South or North, ours all (all, all, all, finally dear to me) - or East or West - Atlantic coast or Mississippi valley - somewhere they crawl'd to die, alone, in bushes, low gullies, or on the sides of hills -

In "Vigil Strange," the poet, perhaps reacting to these thoughts of slain soldiers abandoned or forgotten where they fell, writes of passing the night on the battlefield with a dead comrade in a fraternal communion that defies death:

> **Found you in death so cold dear comrade, ...**
>
> . . . . .
>
> **Long there and then in vigil I stood,**
> **dimly around me the battlefield spreading.**
>
> . . . . .
>
> **Passing sweet hours, immortal and mystic hours with you**
> **dearest comrade - not a tear, not a word,. ..**

Whitman's affection for the fallen soldier is typically his own. Its full emotion is a great outpouring of the pure spirit of human love:

**Vigil of silence, love and death, vigil for you
my son and my soldier,**

. . . . .

**I faithfully loved you and cared for you living,
I think we shall surely meet again,)**

. . . . .

**My comrade I wrap in his blanket, envelop'd well his
form,**

. . . . .

**And there and then and bathed by the rising sun,
my son in his grave, in his rude-dug grave I deposited,**

. . . . .

And buried him where he fell.

The dead comrade is the symbol of all the fallen soldiers. The care taken in his burial is that same care in death that the poet administered to the living wounded in the hospitals of Washington. Whitman's gentle compassion for the soldiers, whom he sees as both comrades and sons, extends beyond life and appears to reach even beyond the grave.

"THE WOUND-DRESSER"

Whitman's attitude toward the troops that he met during the war was brotherly and fatherly; at times it was almost motherly in its tenderness. However, his "love" for these soldiers rises above the abnormal masculine attachment that we have seen previously. While the poet's intense fondness for "our dear darlings" may have had roots in homosexual affections, the war had purified it into a humanitarian compassion. While perhaps excessive, it was elevated above the "manly" relationships suggested in the *Calamus* poems. That part of Whitman's nature which ardently desired great and lasting comradeship discovered satisfaction in the care of the sick and wounded. The common cause for the preservation of the Union contained an ideal climate for the expression of his love of democracy and his deep affection for all his fellow men. The war gave Whitman a very real opportunity to unify and express those emotions which had, up until that time, found a voice only in personal abnormality or in his poetry. "The Wound-Dresser" is an emotional expression of all that Whitman felt in his care of the wounded and dying soldiers. The poem does not focus on the present, but projects the poet into the future, where - with something of the character of a reminiscing veteran - he recalls the war years for the questioning young people around him:

> **An old man bending,**
> **I come among new faces,**
> **Years looking backward resuming in answer**
> **to children, . . .**

The poet is no longer that loud and heated patriot of the early *Drum-Taps* poetry, who shouted:

> **War! an arm'd race is advancing! the welcome for battle,**
> **no turning away; . . .**

In the reality of war, the poet found personal reward not in violent participation, but in the gentle caring for the injured or in a "vigil by the dead:

> **(Arous'd and angry, I'd thought to bent the alarum,**
> **and urge relentless war,**
> **But soon my fingers fail'd me, my face droop'd**
> **and I resign'd myself,**
> **To sit by the wounded and sooth them,**
> **or silently watch the dead;) . . .**

In his vision of the war as recollected in old age, in "dreams' projections," the violent differences between northern and southern causes seem to soften and balance in the "old" poet's memory.

> **Of unsurpass'd heroes, (was one side so brave?**
> **the other was equally brave;) . . .**

From this imagined reverie, Whitman invites those who may inquire to journey back with him in memory to those times when he ministered to the wounded and the dying. Wisely, he warns that the experience is not a pleasant one.

> **With hinged knees returning I enter the doors,**
> **(while for you up there,**
> **Whoever you are, follow without noise and be of strong heart.)**

Whitman relives his nursing rounds through the grim wards of the Union army hospital:

> **Bearing the bandages, water and sponge,**
> **Straight and swift to my wounded I go,**

> . . . . .
>
> To each and all one after another I draw near, not one do I miss,
>
> . . . . .
>
> The crush'd head I dress, (poor crazed hand tear not the bandage away,)
> The neck of the cavalry-man with the bullet through and through I examine,
>
> . . . . .
>
> I am faithful, I do not give out, . . .

Whitman appears to rise in self-exultation as he moves "through the hospitals." The outflowing of brotherly and humanitarian love makes the poet glow with the radiance of a religious healer. No wound or disease among the troops is offensive enough to overcome him. His compassionate love for the troops has the character of a consuming zeal:

> These and more I dress with impassive hand,
> (yet deep in my breast a fire, a burning flame.)

Whitman tends to supercharge the impact of his hospital experiences and to add more than a little dramatic color. However, the intense emotion is not merely vivid poetry; it is also a strong but sensitive confession by the poet. A comparison of part of a letter written to his mother from Washington in 1864 with the final lines of "The Wound-Dresser" will indicate clearly how personal a statement much of the *Drum-Taps* poetry was. The excerpt from the letter reads:

> Mother, I have been in the midst of suffering & death for two months worse than ever - the only comfort is that I have been the cause of some beams of sunshine upon their suffering & gloomy souls & bodies too - many of the dying I have been with too -

Part of the final section of "The Wound-Dresser" contains this same warm expression and sense of dedication to his work:

> The hurt and the wounded I pacify with soothing hand,
> I sit by the restless all the dark night, some are so young,
> Some suffer so much, I recall the experience sweet and sad, . . .

Earlier in the poem, "in dreams' projections," the poet is questioned by the "maidens and young men":

> Of those armies so rapid so wondrous what saw you to tell us?
> What stays with you latest and deepest? . . .

The final two lines of the poem supply the answer. The exchange of tender love, the reaching out of Whitman to the wounded and their clinging to him, are the things preserved in his memory.

> (Many a soldier's loving arms about this neck have crossed and rested,
> Many a soldier's kiss dwells on these bearded lips.)

"GIVE ME THE SPLENDID SILENT SUN"

With the exception of several direct references to the war, this poem bears little resemblance to what we have become accustomed to expect in *Drum-Taps*. The poem has two divisions, laid out in a rhetorical pattern that creates good balance. Whitman was fond of rhetorical movement in his poetry. We have seen flashes of it here and there and, in a concentrated way, in "Song of Myself". In this poem, he creates a mounting emotional tone by the repetition (a Whitman characteristic) of the words "Give me!" at the beginning of the first eleven lines. Here, the poet professes his attraction to the simple, rustic type of natural existence, fundamental and uncomplicated in its pattern:

> Give me the splendid silent sun with
> all its beams full-dazzling,
>
> . . . . .
>
> Give me odorous at sunrise a garden of beautiful
> flowers where I can walk undisturb'd,
> Give me for marriage a sweet-breath'd woman of
> whom
> I should never tire.
> Give me a perfect child, give me away aside from
> the noise of the world a rural domestic life,
>
> . . . . .
>
> Give me solitude, give me Nature, give me again
> O Nature your primal sanities!

At the height of his emotional yearning for the natural existence, the poet shifts from what appeared to be unshakeable ground and turns his attention and affection toward the city - toward "Manhattan."

Despite his almost prayerful demand for "juicy autumnal fruit" and sights of "serene-moving animals teaching content," the poet is "enchain'd" to his "city":

While yet incessantly asking still I adhere to my city,
. . .

He turns his back on the tranquility and embraces the pulse and excitement of his Manhattan:

(O I see what I sought to escape, confronting, reversing my cries,
I see my own soul trampling down what it ask'd for.)

The second section of the poem begins with a commanding rejection of those very pleasures of nature that the poet had honored so enthusiastically at the beginning. The effect rhetorically balances the first few lines of section one:

Keep your splendid silent sun,
Keep your woods O Nature,
and the quiet places by the woods, . . .

From nature's "primal sanities," Whitman cries for the noisy press of the city:

Give me such shows - give me the streets of Manhattan!
Give me Broadway, with the soldiers marching -
give me the sound of the trumpets and drums!

. . . . .

> The life of the theatre, bar-room, . . .
> People, endless, streaming, with strong voices,
> passions, pageants, . . .

The poem is bound to *Drum-Taps* by an atmosphere of extra bustle and excitement in the city during wartime; but the essential **theme** is the question of the two opposite ways of life beckoning to the poet. He must choose between the peace and rustic charm of nature and "Manhattan streets with their powerful throbs." It is the vitality of the city and "an intense life, full of repletion and varied!" that the poet chooses. In the final lines of the poem, Whitman commits himself to his city with finality:

> **Manhattan crowds. With their turbulent musical chorus!**
> **Manhattan faces and eyes forever for me.**

POEMS OF FAREWELL

Several passages from the concluding poems in *Drum-Taps* seem to express Whitman's parting message to the war and to his beloved troops:

> **I have nourish'd the wounded and sooth'd**
> **many a dying soldier,**
> **And at intervals waiting or in the midst of camp,**
> **Composed these songs.**

"Not Youth Pertains to Me"

To the dead he offers a farewell uncolored by Union and Confederate rivalries:

> For my enemy is dead, a man as divine as myself
> is dead,
> I look where he lies white-faced and still in the coffin
> -
> I draw near,
> Bend down and touch lightly with my lips
> the white face in the coffin.

"Reconciliation"

He wishes the force of what he has seen to live on in his poems so that the future may know and understand it:

> Spirit whose work is done -
> spirit of dreadful hours!

. . . . .

> Leave me your pulses of rage - bequeath them to me -
> fill me with current convulsive,
> Let them scorch and blister out of my chants
> when you are gone,
> Let them identify you to the future in these songs.

"Spirit Whose Work is Done"

Whitman bids farewell to the common soldier whose grim ordeals he shared in spirit:

> Adieu O soldier,
> You of the rude campaigning, (which we shared,)

. . . . .

> The hot contention of opposing fronts,
> the long maneuver, . . .

"Adieu to a Soldier"

With the Civil War behind him, and with "peace restored," Whitman faces the future and once again assumes his role as the voice of America and all her peoples, "to the South and to the North." No sectional interests divide the poet's affection. He gives credit to the South for providing, in his wartime activities there, the necessary enrichment for the growth of his future poems:

> The Northern ice and rain that
> began me nourish me to the end,
> But the hot sun of the South is to fully ripen my songs.

"To the Leaven'd Soil They Trod"

This final poem by Whitman reunites in verse the two halves of the nation and supplies a hopeful rededication to the task of singing his democratic and patriotic "chants."

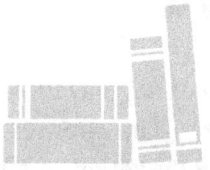

OUT OF THE CRADLE ENDLESSLY ROCKING

BACKGROUND

"Out of the Cradle" is considered to be one of Whitman's finest poems. When it first appeared in a New York literary magazine in 1859, "Out of the Cradle" was entitled "A Child's Reminiscence." Later, in 1860, Whitman incorporated it into the third edition of Leaves and altered the title to "A Word Out of the Sea." By 1871 the poet had made revisions, and the poem appeared with the title by which we know it today.

When we look at the three separate titles and the order of their selection, there appears to be a progression of meanings, each more profound than the one preceding. A simple title such as "A Child's Reminiscence" seems a long way from the heavy implications of "Out of the Cradle Endlessly Rocking." As an **elegy**, the poem is meditative and expresses great lamentation. Critics have differed in attempting to discover biographical origins for the poem. They suggest that some tragic personal loss in Whitman's life may have prompted the poet's reflection upon love and death. Some critics detect a tragic love affair in the poet's past that found expression in such an important part of the poem as the mockingbird's lament.

Whatever the source may have been, the poem remains as a Whitman masterpiece. The **themes** of life, love, and death are not new in the poet's verse; but his handling of them in this poem and in "When Lilacs Last in the Dooryard Bloom'd" indicates a marked growth in poetic craftsmanship in those years following the Civil War. Neither this poem nor "Lilacs" is as long as "Starting from Paumanok" or the enormous "Song of Myself," but they maintain a sustained beauty and order that were not in his previous work. We can always point to these two poems as the high points of Whitman's poetic genius.

THE "PRE-VERSE"

The poem commences with a single sentence of twenty-one lines in which the poet is drawn back in memory to a mysterious childhood experience on the shore of Long Island. Whitman called this section the "Pre-Verse." In it we see the figure of the poet as a boy. The second and much longer section of "Out of the Cradle" was called "Reminiscence" by Whitman, and here he attains in mature recollection an understanding denied to the child on the "Paumanok" beach.

In these first twenty-one lines, there is a curious tapestry of experience. The motion of the section is that of the sea, the life giver, rocking "endlessly." The song that rises "Out of the mocking-bird's throat" seems unified with the voice of the sea in uttering some mysterious meaning or truth. Whitman's Quaker background appears in his use of terminology for the months of the year. On a September night - "the Ninth-month midnight" - the boy is drawn down to the

> **... sterile sands and the fields beyond,**
> **where the child leaving his bed wander'd alone,**

bareheaded, barefoot, . . .

The atmosphere of dreamlike mystery is maintained by Whitman in the

. . . mystic play of shadows twining and twisting as if they were alive, . . .

The poet recalls the song of the mockingbird rising

Out from the patches of briers and blackberries, . . .

His "reminiscence" develops from the bird's three bursts of song and from the pulsing swells of the sea:

**From the memories of the bird that chanted to me,
From your memories sad brother, from the fitful risings and fallings I heard, . . .**

A great mixture of images and impressions appears, which suggests deeper, more mysterious meanings:

**From under that yellow half-moon late-risen and swollen as if with tears,
From those beginning notes of yearning and love there in the mist,
From the thousand responses of my heart never to cease,
From the word stronger and more delicious than any, . . .**

Whitman's reminiscence is strongly suggestive. When "the word" in this last line is identified later in the poem, the mysterious experience on the beach will be fully understood by the poet.

THE "REMINISCENCE"

Whitman had a "musical passion" and a "theatrical one," and often recollected the many performances that he attended during the "splendid seasons of Italian Opera." Critics have compared the bird songs in "Out of the Cradle" and in "Lilacs" with operatic arias. Whitman himself used the term "aria" in "Out of the Cradle." In serious dramatic music, an aria is an ornate melody sung by a solo voice, usually to a musical accompaniment. The mockingbird's **theme** of love and lamentation is typical of the aria. While there is no actual musical accompaniment present in "Out of the Cradle," the surging and muffled roar of the sea seems an adequate substitute.

Whitman's presentation of the bird's three songs is, of course, highly dreamlike and fantastic. By this we mean that he combines the warbling of the bird with his own emotions; in his imagination, he translates the two into the words of poetry.

The narrative, or "Reminiscence," portion of the poem begins with the introduction of

> Two feather'd guests from Alabama, two together, . . .

They are two mockingbirds, the "he-bird" and the "she bird"; the boy observes them near their nest. It is May, the Quaker "Fifth-month"; the grass is springing up and the fragrance of lilacs is in the air. The lilac symbolizes love in Whitman's poetry, and we have seen previously the constant image of the grass in its symbolic representation of life. Love and life are present as the boy, unobserved, watches the two birds and seeks to understand the truths of nature that they represent.

> And every day I, a curious boy, never too close, never disturbing them,
> Cautiously peering, absorbing, translating.

In "Starting From Paumanok," Whitman spoke of having

> . . . walk'd in Alabama my morning walk,
> I have seen where the she-bird the mocking-bird sat on her nest
>
> . . . . .
>
> I have seen the he-bird also,
> I have paus'd to hear him near at hand inflating his throat and joyfully singing.
> And while I pause'd it came to me what he really sang for was not there only,
> Nor for his mate nor himself only, nor all sent back by the echoes,
> But subtle, clandestine, away beyond,
> A charge transmitted and gift occult for those being born.

This earlier use of the mockingbird image is significant for our examination of "Out of the Cradle." The poet's awareness of a deeper meaning beneath the appearances of nature is the same sensation he experiences as a boy on the Long Island beach, but understands only in mature reflection.

At first the male mockingbird's song in "Out of the Cradle" gaily announces the happiness shared by him and his mate:

> Shine! shine! shine!
> Pour down your warmth, great sun!
> While we bask, we two together.

> . . . . .

> Singing all time, minding no time, . . .

The lyrical cry of the bird is interrupted by the voice of the poet, who tells us that, on one occasion, he failed to see the "she-bird" in her nest; she never appeared again. The restless male mockingbird, "the solitary guest" on the beach, wails the loss of his mate and cries for her return:

> Blow up sea-winds along Paumanok's shore;
> I wait and I wait till you blow my mate to me.

Whitman's reminiscence sees the mournful bird as "the lone singer wonderful causing tears." The poet shifts back and forth in time. At first he observes the bird with boyish wonder. Then in maturity he ponders over the meaning of what he saw and heard years ago.

> Yes my brother I know,
> The rest might not, but I have treasur'd every note,

> . . . . .

> I, with bare feet, a child, the wind wafting my hair,
> Listen'd long and long.

The song of the bird was well remembered; only now can its meaning be understood.

Listen'd to keep, to sing, now translating the notes,
...

The song of the mockingbird is heavy with love and loneliness. The bird cries out for his lost mate and ends with mournful despair:

This gentle call is for you my love, for you.

.....

Loved! loved! loved! loved! loved!
But my mate no more, no more with me!
We two together no more.

As the "aria" of the bird comes to an end, Whitman's reminiscence visualizes himself ("The boy ecstatic"), the sea ("the fierce old mother incessantly moaning"), and the mockingbird as a "trio." The sea and the bird, "each uttering," have a message for him. They speak "To the outsetting bard," to the boy who will become the poet and now seeks answers to his "soul's questions." In his reflection, the poet addresses the bird as "Demon" and asks:

Is it indeed toward your mate you sing? Or is it really to me?
For I, that was a child, my tongue's use sleeping, now I have heard you, ...

To the boy who was the future poet, the bird was a "Demon," an inspiring spirit, teaching the notion of love which is now examined in mature reflection. The cries of love by the mockingbird ignited the boy's emotion, to be poetically fulfilled in adulthood and never to be forgotten.

> Now in a moment I know what I am for, I awake,

> . . . . .

> A thousand warbling echoes have started to life within me, never to die.

Whitman addresses the mockingbird as

> O you singer solitary, singing by yourself, projecting me, . . .

In "Starting from Paumanok," he created a similar image indicating his poetic role. He confessed to "having heard the mocking-bird's tones," and added that

> Solitary, singing in the West, I strike up for a New World.

Thus, in "Out of the Cradle" the bird in his lonely song "projects" the boy's future vocation of poet. Whitman, the man, now comprehends the full significance of the bird's song, which he had only vaguely sensed before.

> O solitary me listening, never more shall I cease perpetuating you,

> . . . . .

> The messenger there arous'd, the fire, the sweet hell within,
> The unknown want, the destiny of me.

THE SEA RESPONDS

In the "Pre-Verse" section of the poem, Whitman spoke of "the word stronger and more delicious than any." However, the bird's message of "lonesome love" is not enough; it is not

The final word, superior to all, . . .

It is from the sea, "the savage old mother," that the answer must come. Throughout the poem we have been conscious of the "undertone" of the sea in the background, "incessantly crying." The sea holds the ultimate "word" that the poet seeks. The bird cried only of love, but that love was "lonesome" and unfulfilled; the "singer" was left incomplete by the loss of its mate. The sea, violent, yet motherly and gentle,

Delaying not, hurrying not,

. . . . .

Lisp'd to me the low and delicious word death,
And again death, death, death, death,
Hissing melodiously, neither like the bird nor like my
arous'd child's heart,

. . . . .

Creeping thence steadily up to my ears and laving me softly all over,
Death, death, death, death, death, . . .

The sea is the "mother," wiser than both bird and boy, the symbol of birth. By whispering the word "Death," the sea gives life's essential meaning to the poet. "The word of the sweetest song," that "strong and delicious word," death, coming from the sea, reveals that life and death are balancing functions in the universe, with death leading to rebirth. The "carols of lonesome love" sung by the mockingbird could not blend the two ideas; the wise "old mother," the sea, can:

> ... like some old crone rocking the cradle, swathed
> in sweet garments, bending aside,)
> **The sea whisper'd me.**

The poet is now aware of the pattern of life and death. He will "fuse the song" of the bird with the message from the sea, "the word up from the waves."

> **With the thousand responsive songs at random,**
> **My own songs awaked from that hour,** ...

Thus, Whitman has been illuminated and has attained poetic maturity through this understanding of life's ultimate meaning.

SUMMARY

The poem represents essentially the passage from childhood questioning and curiosity to a philosophic and poetic maturity. In reflection, the poet recalls a haunting childhood experience on the beaches of Long Island. With fascination, he had cautiously watched two mockingbirds who had nested on the shore. One day, the female bird did not return, and the boy listened to the lonesome song of the male for his lost mate. Now, as an adult, the poet recalls the song and translates into words the emotion that the bird's lamentation conveyed to him. The cry of "lonesome love" inspired in him a love "tumultuously bursting" like that of the mockingbird, and awakened in him his vocation of poet.

However, an understanding of this kind of love was not sufficient. The bird's lament was for a lost love, and the creature was empty and despairing in his grief. There was no resolution of love, death and life in his "carol." The final and complete understanding of the life-death rhythm and cyclic pattern of existence is whispered by the sea.

The answer, the "delicious word," is whispered by the eternal "mother." The maternal sea utters a message of death, which is only understood years later in the poet's manhood. Thus, Whitman sees that death and life are bound together and are not opposites in the order of things. The poet sees what the bird could not in its song - that in death there is life, and a loss to death is ultimately a movement to life in rebirth. This is the meaning of life for Whitman, and it brings him to full poetic maturity. As the sea whispered "death," it also whispered a message of life.

At the end of the poem, the yearning for understanding resolves into calm assurance. The "old crone rocking the cradle, swathed in sweet garments" softly blends the ideas of life and death. In the final comprehension of life's meaning, there is no longer any anxiety for the poet.

WHEN LILACS LAST IN THE DOORYARD BLOOM'D

BACKGROUND

Whitman's *Sequel to Drum-Taps* was issued in 1865 and included four elegies on President Lincoln. The most famous of these is "When Lilacs Last in the Dooryard Bloom'd." Along with "Out of the Cradle," it represents Whitman's greatest poetry and is recognized as one of the high points of American verse. The "Lilacs" **elegy** is an outpouring of the deep sense of loss that Whitman felt after the assassination of President Abraham Lincoln. In *Specimen Days*, a prose collection of "diary-jottings" and "war-memoranda," Whitman recollects two of the most memorable events of the war - and certainly of his life:

> (Of all the days of the war, there are two especially I can never forget. Those were the day following the news, in New York and Brooklyn, of that first Bull Run defeat, and the day of Abraham Lincoln's death. I was home in Brooklyn on both occasions. The day of the murder we heard the news very early in the morning. Mother prepared breakfast . . . not a mouthful was eaten all day by either of us . . . Little was said . . . .)

The President's death was a great shock to the poet; it overwhelmed him in a very personal way. In another selection from *Specimen Days*, we can see how clearly Whitman recognized Lincoln's excellence and importance:

> . . . the greatest, best, most characteristic, artistic, moral personality . . . The tragic splendor of his death, purging, illuminating all, throws round his form, his head, an aureole, [a type of bright halo] that will remain and will grow brighter through time, while history lives, and lover of country lasts. . . .

On April 15, 1865, the President was dead. His death produced the superb statement of Whitman's emotions - "When Lilacs Last in the Dooryard Bloom'd."

A TRINITY OF SYMBOLS

When Whitman first heard of the assassination, it was the spring of the year and the lilacs were in bloom.

> When lilacs last in the dooryard bloom'd,
> And the great star early droop'd
> in the western sky in the night,
> I mourn'd, and yet shall mourn with ever-returning spring.
> Ever-returning spring, trinity sure to me you bring,
> Lilac blooming perennial and drooping star in the west,
> And thought of him I love.

The poem is heavily symbolic. In this first section, Whitman introduces two of the three central symbols used in development.

The poet appears in company with the "Lilac blooming" and the "drooping star." The lilac represents love as well as resurrection and rebirth ("blooming perennial"). It should also be noted that in the symbolism of the eastern countries, the flower is associated with the idea of manly love. The star symbolizes the slain Abraham Lincoln and comes to symbolize, also, the poet's heavy grief for him. The star, or Lincoln, once celestial and shining like a strong guide to those beneath it, has now "droop'd early." Lincoln is dead, fallen like a great and radiant body from the heavens.

The idea of death is constantly woven in with the **theme** of rebirth throughout the poem. The poet mourns and "shall mourn" with the arrival of spring. Spring, with its character of rebirth and life, will bring reminders of the dead Lincoln - "thought of him I love."

Section 1 is a great lamentation for the "fallen star," but the poet's emotional fervor borders on the overly dramatic:

> **O powerful western fallen star!**
> **O shades of night - O moody, tearful night!**
> **O great star disappear'd - O the black murk that hides the star!**
> **O cruel hands that hold me powerless - O helpless soul of me!**
> **O harsh surrounding cloud that will not free my soul.**

The **stanza** contains the symbols of the heavy grief that weighs upon the poet. The "shades of night, . . . the black murk" and "harsh surrounding cloud" press upon Whitman like a pall separating him from the "fallen" Lincoln. The mood of "Lilacs" is somber, appropriate for an **elegy**; but the sense of sorrow is never particularized. Nowhere in the poem is Lincoln's name even mentioned. There is no sense of positive location, and the grief expressed in the poem seems suspended in time. The heavy symbolism allows for a philosophical consideration of death and permits a lamentation great enough to represent the grief of the entire nation.

In **section 1** Whitman spoke of

Ever-returning spring, trinity sure to me you bring,
...

We have seen the lilac and the star as two parts of that "trinity." **Section 4** supplies the final member:

In the swamp in secluded recesses,
A shy and hidden bird is warbling a song.
Solitary the thrush,
The hermit withdrawn to himself, avoiding the settlements,
Sings by himself a song.

Whitman has now introduced and begun to extend the three primary symbolic tools by which he will develop the **elegy** - the "lilac," the "star," and the "thrush." The star symbol, extended into **Section 2**, is concealed from view by three minor symbols of gloom - the "night," the "murk," and the "cloud" - acting like "cruel hands." Therefore, within a part of the main "trinity" of symbols, Whitman employs a lesser trinity.

The lilac image is continued into **Section 3**, producing "heart-shaped leaves" with blossoms "rising delicate," and "every leaf a miracle." The blossoms and the leaves are symbols of love, birth, and eternal rebirth, **themes** which we recognize as persistent in Whitman's work.

Like "Out of the Cradle," this poem presents the figure of a bird singing an "aria" or "carol." Unlike the lonely love song of the mockingbird, the "solitary . . . thrush" warbles a lyrical lament on death that invites an understanding and acceptance of it. In "Out of the Cradle," the bird's song was inadequate for a comprehension of the pattern of life and death; the answer finally came from the whispering sea. In "Lilacs," the inviting thrush contains all the answers that the mockingbird lacked and that the sea finally revealed. In the thrush's song in "Lilacs," there is also the echo of the poet's uncontrollable need to voice his own sorrow:

> **Song of the bleeding throat,**
> **Death's outlet song of life, (for well dear brother I know,**
> **If thou wast not granted to sing thou would'st surely die.)**

DOUBLE MOVEMENT

In **section 5**, the funeral train bearing Lincoln's body moves across the country toward Springfield, Illinois, where the murdered President is to be buried.

> **Over the breast of the spring, the land, amid cities,**
>
> . . . . .
>
> **Carrying a corpse to where it shall rest in the grave,**
> **Night and day journeys a coffin.**

We are now prepared for a double movement in the poem. Whitman will proceed from his first condition of utter dejection toward a final adjustment to the idea of the President's death. The passage of Lincoln's body in its mournful, measured pace across the country parallels the philosophical journey of the poet from despair to resignation and acceptance of the loss of "the sweetest, wisest soul of all my days and lands."

In **Section 6**, the "silent sea of faces: across the states watch as Lincoln's coffin passes through their cities on its way to Illinois. Except for the muffled "dirges," the mournful onlookers are silent. The nation's grief is evident everywhere.

Coffin that passes through lanes and streets,
Through day and night with the great cloud darkening the land, ...

As the dead President is borne along, the poet offers his humble but symbolic tribute:

Here, coffin that slowly passes,
I give you my sprig of lilac.

It is the symbol of love and resurrection that the poet extends. It is an offering of simple beauty and rich significance to the man whose great appeal lay partly in an image of classic American simplicity, a president of whom Whitman would remark in his chant *Specimen Days*, "Mr. Lincoln ... looks as ordinary in attire ... as the commonest man...."

In **Sections 7** and **8**, Whitman's "sprig" multiplies:

Blossoms and branches green to coffins all I bring, ...

He has given a token for all the dead, and a "song for you O sane and sacred death":

> All over bouquets of roses,
> ....and early lilies,
> But mostly and now the lilac that blooms the first,...

Whitman's gesture symbolizes love and grief, but the lilac that "blooms the first" is a hopeful symbol of rebirth. It should be remembered that for Whitman death is not the enemy with whom there can be no ultimate peace. However, the complete, acceptance of Lincoln's death remains for the end of the poem and is to be reached only after an intense struggle with personal grief.

In **Section 8**, Whitman addresses the evening star that he had observed "a month" previously:

> O western orb sailing the heaven,
> Now I know what you must have meant as a month since I walk'd,
>
> . . . . .
>
> As I saw you had something to tell as you bent to me night after night, . . .

The message, the "something to tell," was the death of Lincoln; and the somber passage of the "orb" across the evening sky was a foreshadowing parallel of the President's journey in death across the country.

THE POET'S STRUGGLE WITH GRIEF

In **Section 9**, the mourning poet is pulled in two directions. The swamp thrush, the "singer bashful and tender," calls the poet to an understanding of death's proper place in creation, and, thereby, an acceptance of Lincoln's death in the pattern of nature. However, the ultimate acceptance must be delayed a while.

> **I hear, I come presently, I understand you,**
> **But a moment I linger, for the lustrous star has detain'd me,**
> **The star my departing comrade holds and detains me.**

We know now that the poet will finally be united with the warble of the bird. The star, representing both the "comrade" Lincoln and the poet's grief, monopolizes Whitman's thoughts and will. After a while, he will answer the thrush's summons to the ultimate resolution of his grief and Lincoln's loss in the idea of death; but he will indulge that grief for the "moment." The pause and the hesitant willingness to release the murdered President to death persist through **Sections 10**, **11**, and **12**, as the poet ponders the problem involved in mourning for Lincoln. How can his song of mourning, a song breathed out with the breath of life, be adequate for someone who is dead - how can it express his emotion for "the large sweet soul that has gone?"

> **O how shall I warble myself for the dead one there I loved?**
>
> . . . . .
>
> **And what shall my perfume be for the grave of him I love?**

There is a second problem delaying the poet from fully embracing the call of the thrush:

O what shall I hang on the chamber walls?
And what shall the pictures be that I hang on the walls,
To adorn the burial-house of him I love?

Both questions involve Whitman's temporary inability, or unwillingness, to accept the President's death. The answers are supplied by the poet himself in a way that brings him closer to reconciliation and acceptance of the fact. To the question of "how shall I warble myself . . . ?", he responds in terms that suggest activity and life, not finality in death:

Sea-winds blown from east and west,

. . . . .

These and with these and the breath of my chant,
I'll perfume the grave of him I love.

The wind, the breath of nature, and his own living breath are suitable for the task.

What would be proper to adorn the house of the dead, the place where the body of the lost "comrade" will lie? Once again, Whitman's solution does not contain signs and ornaments implying death's finality. Upon the "chamber walls," the adornments are symbols of life and rebirth:

Pictures of growing spring and farms and homes,

. . . . .

With floods of the yellow gold of the
gorgeous indolent, sinking sun, . . .

> With the fresh sweet herbage under foot, . . .
>
> . . . . .
>
> And the city at hand with dwellings so dense,
> and stacks of chimneys, . . .

To the tomb of the President, the poet will bring "all the scenes of life." By this act, the ideas of life and death, which had seemed irreconcilable in Whitman's grief, move closer together. However, he is still not prepared to accept completely the fact of Lincoln's death and the proper place of death itself in the order of nature. Behind the hesitation and gradual movement of the poet towards that realization, we are constantly aware of the presence of the "singer bashful and tender," the hidden bird, patient and insistent, waiting in the background.

> Sing on, sing on you gray-brown bird,
> Sing from the swamps, recesses, . . .
>
> . . . . .
>
> Sing on dearest brother, warble your reedy song,
>
> . . . . .
>
> O wild and loose to my soul -
> O wondrous singer!
> You only I hear - yet the star holds me,
> (but will soon depart),
> Yet the lilac with mastering odor holds me.

The thrush's call to the acceptance of death is continued. It is not that Whitman's tarrying over Lincoln's memory represents an unshakable refusal or denial of death as a natural principle. Rather, it is simply hesitation and postponement of that inevitable acceptance, a reluctance prompted by grief. After the interruption by the thrush's call, the "pictures" continue to appear in **Section 14**. It should be noted also that these tokens of honor that Whitman considers appropriate for Lincoln's "burial-house" are not the priceless tributes usually associated with a fallen head of state. Actually, they are very plain tributes, "pictures" of everyday scenes that are quite ordinary in appearance.

> ... the fields of spring, and the
> farmers preparing their crops,
> In the large unconscious scenery of my land
> with its lakes and forests,
>
> . . . . .
>
> And the streets how their throbbings throbb'd, ...

These scenes, which have appeared in **Sections 11, 12, and 14**, are the "pictures" of America - the very things that Lincoln represented and defended as President. In their rich simplicity, they appropriately honor his humble greatness.

THE LAMENT OF THE THRUSH

Section 14 contains Whitman's encounter with two "companions":

> Then with the knowledge of death
> as walking one side of me,
> And the thought of death close -

> walking the other side of me,
> And I in the middle as with companions, ...

He has been joined by an understanding of what death is ("knowledge of death"), in company with his awareness of the loss of someone dear to him ("thought of death"). They form another type of trinity and hasten on

> To the solemn shadowy cedars and ghostly pines so still.
> And the singer so shy to the rest receiv'd me,
> The gray-brown bird I know receiv'd us comrades three,
> And he sang the carol of death, and a verse for him I love.

Whitman is now fully united with the reality and complete acceptance of death, as the "carol of the bird" engulfs his whole being:

> And the charm of the carol rapt me,
>
> . . . . .
>
> And the voice of my spirit tallied the song of the bird.

The thrush carries Whitman along in a hymn of praise to death, the

> Dark mother always gliding near with soft feet, ...

The song of praise swells in a fluid movement, drawing Whitman into compatible union with it. There is a somber, smothering softness that calms the poet's reluctance of release the thought of the dead Lincoln to "the sure-enwinding arms of cool-enfolding death."

In the bird's chant, death is desirable, a mighty and noble comforter and a place of rest. How like the whispering sea in "Out of the Cradle," with its life-death message, is Whitman's image of death in "Lilacs":

> **Approach strong deliveress,**
> **When it is so, when thou hast taken them**
> **I joyously sing the dead,**
> **Lost in the loving floating ocean of thee,**
> **Laved in the flood of thy bliss O death.**

As **Section 14** ends, the song of the thrush rises in delight to salute death. There is no heavy grief here - no "dirges pour'd around the coffin," nor "cities drapped in black," nor "crapeveil'd women standing." The real "knowledge" of death, at which the poet has arrived by coming to the thrush, is a place where death is addressed in a "chant of fullest welcome." The song of the bird proposes "glad serenades" for death: "Dances for thee . . . feastings for thee, . . .the sights of the open landscape and the high-spread sky are fitting."

VISION AND FINAL UNION

In harmonious union with the bird's "carol," the poet's "soul" moves forward into the "panoramas of visions" of **Section 15**:

> **To the tally of my soul,**
> **Loud and strong kept up the gray-brown bird,**
>
> . . . . .

> While my sight that was bound in my eyes unclosed,
>
> . . . . .
>
> I saw the debris and debris of all the
> slain soldiers of the war, . . .

The poet realizes that death has brought bliss to those who died in the Civil War. Like the farm mother in "Come up From the Fields Father," the survivors and the families really endure pain and sufferings:

> But I saw they were not as was thought,
> They themselves were fully at rest, they suffer'd not,
> The living remain'd and suffer'd, the mother suffer'd, . . .

In the final section of the poem, Whitman takes leave of the "visions" - of all those things that have brought him to an understanding of death. He departs from his "comrades" who were the "knowledge" of death and the "thought" of death: "the song of the hermit bird," the "lilac with the heart-shaped leaves," and the star that the poet addresses as

> O comrade lustrous with silver face in the night.

However, in departing from them, Whitman does not reject the lilac and the star, the earthly love and the sadness he felt for the departed. These symbols, which gave way to the song of the thrush and its message of peaceful acceptance and resolution, are not abandoned. They are united, at the end of the poem, in the poet's philosophical understanding of the place of all three in the natural order of things, and in his willingness to release his beloved Lincoln to the "Dark mother" of the thrush's song.

> For the sweetest, wisest soul of all my days and lands
> - . . .
> Lilac and star and bird twined with the chant of my soul, . . .

SUMMARY AND COMPARISON

"When Lilacs Last" is an **elegy** on the death of Abraham Lincoln as well as a philosophical poem on death itself. Through the symbolic use of a star, a lilac, and a bird, the poet journeys through grieving love to a final acceptance of death. In spite of the involved symbolism, Whitman's method of arriving at the truth of death follows a pattern far less artificial than that in "Song of Myself," and more typically human than the one he pursued in "Out of the Cradle."

The acceptance of Lincoln's death, as well as an understanding of death's place in the human pattern, are attained only after an encounter with love and grief. Whitman does not forsake the mournful sense of loss once the full meaning of immortality and peace in death is understood. He discovers them to be compatible parts of a more complete realization, just as he found life, love, and death to be interlocking parts of existence in "Out of the Cradle." The jaunty self-assurance of "Song of Myself" is absent. In "Song of Myself," there is no agonized emotional distance to travel for the poet to grasp an understanding of the notions of rebirth and immortality that he finds in death. There is no room for a thoroughly human awareness of grief. In "Out of the Cradle," the grief of the mockingbird is not the poet's personal sorrow that is found in "Lilacs." The treatment of death in "Lilacs" indicates how deeply grieved Whitman was by his war experiences and by Lincoln's assassination. In "Song of Myself," there is no test of the poet's philosophy.

In the Lincoln **elegy**, the poet's beliefs are challenged by exposing the emotions to attack by grief. "Out of the Cradle" presents no test for Whitman's beliefs, but provides growth and understanding with time and maturity.

In "Lilacs," Whitman appears more sober and well balanced. In all three poems, there is an optimistic acceptance of death and understanding of its desirable place in that natural cycle of regeneration we have seen Whitman announce so often.

There is a steady and well-composed order of movement in "Lilacs." The flow is direct; and the poetry, while a bit overly dramatic on occasion, leaves no gaps or unconnected sections of verse as in "Song of Myself." Whitman has attained superb balance with a calm and positive toning down of the poem's pace as he rises to a philosophic awareness. The result is a delicate poise at the end that convinces most critics of the fact that this is one of Whitman's greatest poems, and perhaps his most successful in all respects.

CROSSING BROOKLYN FERRY

....

BACKGROUND

Claimed by Thoreau as his favorite, "Crossing Brooklyn Ferry" is one of Whitman's long poems as well as one of his best developed. It was originally called "Sun Down Poem," in the second edition of *Leaves of Grass* in 1856; the present title was assigned in 1860.

It seems natural that Whitman should have written a poem around the idea of a ferry boat and its trip across a river. He was exhilarated and inspired by the movement and mystery of the sea, and by the "river and bay scenery all about New York island." In *Specimen Days*, Whitman recounts his fascination for ferries and indicates how highly suggestive of deeper meaning were those trips back and forth between Brooklyn and Manhattan:

> **Living in Brooklyn or New York city . . . my life . . . was curiously identified with Fulton ferry, . . . Almost daily, later, ('50, to '60,) I cross'd on the boats, often up in the pilot-houses where I could get a full sweep, absorbing shows, accompaniments, surroundings. What oceanic currents, eddies, underneath - the great tides of humanity also, with ever-shifting**

movements. Indeed, I have always had a passion for ferries; to me they afford inimitable, streaming, never-failing, living poems . . . what refreshment of spirit such sights and experiences gave me years ago (and many a time since).

Walt Whitman was able to translate these sensations into poetry that reflected not only the immediate pleasure he derived from his trips across the open water, but the deeper philosophical symbols that this passage from shore to shore contained for him. "Crossing Brooklyn Ferry" is the presentation of those symbols and the poetical translation of those mysterious sensations that he experienced.

THE FERRY AS A SYMBOL

In the first of the poem's nine sections, Whitman addresses the "Flood-tide below," the "Clouds," and the "sun" above. He addresses the "Crowds of men and women" whose constant movement from shore to shore by ferry is "more curious" to the poet than they imagine. At the end of the first section, Whitman reaches ahead to the future and commences his development of the broader suggestions that the ferry scene contains for him:

> And you that shall cross from shore to shore
> years hence are more to me, and more in my meditations,
> than you might suppose.

We have already seen in other poems Whitman's persistent ideas on the eternal forward movement of all things through life, death and rebirth, and his notions of an interrelationship of all people that transcends time and place. We have seen him reach back to acknowledge the past or look forward to greet the wonderful future. The idea of the ferry's passage from shore to shore fits well symbolically with the poet's notions of an evolving and forward movement in all of nature. The ferry, the people that cross on it, and the rushing water beneath, loom up for Whitman as mystical symbols of a perpetual and unified flow of humanity from the present into the future. The only scene in the poem is New York harbor; therefore, it is a very realistic one. But the poet's meditations expand it into a timeless locale that is part of a dreamlike vision.

> **The current rushing so swiftly and swimming with me**
> **far away,**
> **The others that are to follow me, the ties between me**
> **and them,**
> **. . . . .**
> **Others will enter the gates of the ferry and cross from shore to shore,**
> **Others will watch the run of the flood-tide, . . .**

Whitman develops a double level of meaning. His meditation and ferry crossing may be interpreted at the surface level; that is, he may be considered merely to observe the endless bustle of people and water traffic and sights and sounds of the harbor in an unmystical manner. However, to accept the poem on this basis is to fail to see the richer and more important philosophical meaning that is present.

A STRONG BOND WITH THE FUTURE

In **Section 3**, Whitman extends himself beyond the present and joins with future generations who will experience the same sensations and behold the same sights as he does then:

> **I am with you, you men and women of a generation,**
> **or ever so many generations hence, . . .**

Whitman creates an atmosphere of timelessness by means of a curious blending of the present with the future. He looks ahead from his own time as well as back from a future moment in the company of future people. In a reflection upon himself and what he sees, he breaks down the barriers between time-present and time-future, and unites future generations with his own by the mutual sharing of experience and sensation:

> **Just as you feel when you look on the river and sky,**
> **so I felt,**
> **Just as any of you is one of a living crowd,**
> **I was one of a crowd,**
>
> **. . . . .**
>
> **I too many and many a time cross'd the river of old, . . .**

Much of **Section 3** is taken up with a pictorial catalogue of river and harbor sights. These are an expansion of the shared experiences, the points of communion between Whitman and those future generations he visualizes. He, likewise,

> **Saw the reflection of the summer sky in the water,**
>
> **. . . . .**

Look'd toward the lower bay to notice the vessels arriving,

. . . . .

Saw the white sails of schooners and sloops, saw the ships at anchor,

. . . . .

The round masts, the swinging motion of the hulls, the slender serpentine pennants,
The large and small streamers in motion, the pilots in their pilothouses,
The white wake left by the passage, the quick tremulous
whirl of the wheels,
The flags of all nations, the falling of them at sunset,...

An awareness of time falls away, as the harbor activities that quicken his pulse and inspire him become the same sources of excitement for future observers. The busy sights and sounds could be the bustle of any place and any time: their symbolic meaning transcends the harbor and represents the sharing of all life's experiences. Time and distance never isolate peoples in the philosophy of Whitman's poetry; and never does the poet abandon his belief in a unified chain of humanity, unbroken and extending forward and backward in time.

Several images in **Section 3** suggest notions of a life and death cycle. Gazing from the ferry, Whitman sees the "glistening yellow" of the day. His eyes are "dazzled by the shimmering track of beams." He watches the "spokes of light round the shape of my head in the sunlit water," and witnesses the lowering of ships' flags "at sunset." Through the bright radiance of the day, Whitman passes along in communion with future generations to a sunset at evening. More than the short time lapse of a day, the images with their movement toward sunset suggest the human journey from birth to death and the unity of generations in an endless process.

The catalogue itself is not allowed the boundless freedom that we saw in the catalogues of "Song of Myself." It is more controlled, has equally good pictorial quality, and balances well between the plain, direct description of the busy river scene and the suggestive symbolism that the ferry's movement presents. As a meeting place of experience for the present and the future, this catalogue must be seen as a functional part of the poem. It is not isolated, nor is it overfilled with items as many critics see Whitman's catalogues to be in general. While the catalogue device is a characteristic part of Whitman's poetry, and as such has an indispensable charm and value, many critics maintain that it represents an unsuccessful experiment by the poet. This short catalogue in "Crossing Brooklyn Ferry" is a refined and controlled use of the technique and has the proper proportion to be good poetry.

A SPIRITUAL "FLOAT"

From what Whitman believes to be a great spiritual reservoir, he has been drawn and given individuality:

> **I too had been struck from the float forever held in solution,
> I too had receiv'd identity by my body, . . .**

He "too," like all men, possesses individuality, yet is bound in a unity of common spiritual origin. From that spiritual storehouse, the "float," each person is given bodily form and individuality.

In addition, the poet sees all men sharing the common bonds of their human natures.

> I too knitted the old knot of contrariety,
> Blabb'd, blush'd, resented, lied, stole, grudg'd,
>
> . . . . .
>
> The wolf, the snake, the hog, not wanting in me,
>
> . . . . .
>
> Refusals, hates, postponements, meanness, laziness, none
> of these wanting,
>
> . . . . .
>
> The same old role, the role that is what we make it, as
> great as we like,
> Or as small as we like, or both great and small.

In **section 7**, the poet and his fellow man of the future, unhampered by time, intensify their mutual reflection:

> Closer yet I approach you,
> What thought you have of me now, I had as much of you. . . .

In **Section 8**, Whitman returns to a happy contemplation of his immediate surroundings:

> Ah, what can ever be more stately and admirable to me
> than masthemm'd Manhattan?
> River and sunset and scallop-edg'd waves of flood-tide?

In reality, the ferry transports people from one place to another; poetically, it is symbolic of a movement through life and death toward the future. Whitman's poem serves much the same function but bridges the gap simply and directly.

> What is more subtle than this which ties me to the woman
> or man that looks in my face?
> Which fuses me into you now, and pours my meaning into you?
> We understand then, do we not?

> . . . . .

> What the study could not teach - what the preaching could
> not accomplish is accomplish'd, is it not?

Section 9 is highly oratorical; the poet invokes the "flood-tide," the "waves," the "Gorgeous clouds," "crowds of passengers," the "tall masts of Mannahatta," and even the "beautiful hills of Brooklyn," as he unites images and ideas previously presented in the poem. He seems to pause in an attachment to the experiences and sensations of life but returns to an awareness of the pattern of progress and immortality he has visualized:

> Suspend here and everywhere, eternal float of solution!
> Gaze, loving and thirsting eyes, in the house
> or street or public assembly!
>
> . . . . .
>
> Be firm, rail over the river, to support those who lean
> idly, yet haste with the hasting current; ...

The "sea-birds" who "wheel in large circles" create symbols of the round or full-circle pattern that Whitman sees in all of nature. The repetition of the "sunset" image closes the cycle.

As the poem concludes, Whitman addresses the material objects of the world:

> Keep your places, objects than which none else
> is more lasting.
> You have waited, you always wait, you dumb,
> beautiful ministers, ...

The things of the world have a function; as "ministers," they are helpful to man:

> We use you, and do not cast you aside -
> we plant you permanently within us, ...

However, as with all parts of Whitman's universe, they move "toward eternity" too. They are not central to life but only contribute toward the flow into immortality.

SUMMARY

"Crossing Brooklyn Ferry" is a mature example of Whitman's poetry. The poem has great poise and balanced movement. Whitman's symbols never trample his ideas, and the ideas are never forced from the symbols. In the image of the ferry and its journey from shore to shore lies Whitman's basic philosophy of the great flow of all things through life toward immortality. The past and future are linked to the present in this concept, and the chain is infinite and timeless.

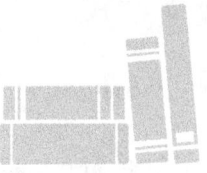

WALT WHITMAN TODAY

The position of Walt Whitman in American literature has been established. Both time and changing social and literary attitudes have brought Whitman to a place from which he cannot be shaken. His shadow may grow momentarily longer or shorter in the sifting process that is critical debate, but his essential stature will not be reduced. What shocked the average reader in 1855 no longer outrages, although Whitman's poetry still manages to offend good taste at times. What confounded the mid-nineteenth century poetry lover in Whitman's verse form now fails to disturb the new reader for very long. It appears as if American literature, after a healthy period of adjustment, has allowed itself to grow into Whitman's poetry. The "good gray poet," who was better than a half-century in advance of his times, has now had the advantage of decades of devoted scholarship that bring his art - but not without persistent problems - before our eyes with greater clarity, and his strange and exciting language within the understanding range of our hearing.

It will be recalled that Whitman was poorly received by the American common man to whom he had directed his poetry. Only a few intellectuals in this country received him well. Men such as Emerson and Thoreau, writers themselves, admired *Leaves of Grass* but not without some reservations. However, Whitman's faith was always in the future; and it was in this future that he sought justification. In his poem "Poets to Come," included in the *Inscriptions* group, Whitman calls out to our times:

> **Poets to come! orators, singers, musicians to come!**
> **Not to-day is to justify me and answer what I am for,**
> **But you, a new brood, native, athletic, continental, greater than before known,**
> **Arouse! for you must justify me.**

Whitman's influence upon modern poetry cannot be denied. Truly modern poets such as Ezra Pound, T. S. Eliot, Hart Crane, Robinson Jeffers, Williams Carlos Williams, and especially Carl Sandburg consciously and unconsciously felt the influence of the Whitman poetic spirit. Ezra Pound, whose own poetry has raised much Whitman-like controversy, does not deny some of the revolting aspects in the poet's work, but perceives Whitman as a successful poet and himself as one of those heralded "Poets to come!"

The American poet and critic Randall Jarrell finds Whitman absurd, improbable and certainly incomparable. Yet, he is enthusiastic about the poet's frankness and boldness; what he sees in Whitman is nobility, scope, and an intense reality in the poetic encounter with life and the world.

The English novelist and poet D. H. Lawrence, who died in 1930, shed some light on the question of the morality of Whitman's poetry. Lawrence saw the man as a great poet of the soul - something like a crusading leader whose poetry was not immoral but was actually a refocusing of morality.

Whatever may be the particular likes and dislikes of critics and poets in our own era, the fact remains that their brisk controversies have stirred up sharp popular interest in Whitman.

For longer than was healthy for American literature, Whitman's beloved average American and almost every schoolboy were acquainted with the poet by no firmer contact than the always-recited and rather sing-songy Lincoln poem, "O Captain! My Captain!" Thankfully, those days are rapidly ending. The great surge of Whitman scholarship, rising from about 1926 to its great momentum of today, is unraveling much of that knot of mystery and puzzlement that barred Whitman for so long from popular acceptance as a great national poet.

One fact about Whitman criticism is boldly evident: critical approaches themselves are acute points of contention. The critic Richard Chase sees Whitman as a thoroughly representative voice of America. The late philosopher and critic George Santayana was convinced that he was no such thing, while Gay Wilson Allen detects in Whitman marked philosophical outgrowths from European sources.

Undeniably, critics feel the personal force of Whitman in his poetry. Even when Whitman appears weakest, we cannot ignore the man's own zest racing through his lines. The poet wished his own person to fill *Leaves of Grass*, and his success in this regard has certainly contributed to the heartiness of his appeal today. Whenever we sit down to read Whitman, it might be wise to pause for a moment at two particular lines in the poem, "So Long!," from the section *Songs at Parting*. There is a message here, a revelation of the very life blood of *Leaves of Grass*, projected timelessly toward Whitman's readers "to come":

Camerado, this is no book,
Who touches this touches a man, . . .

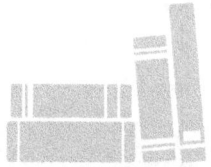

QUESTIONS AND ANSWERS FOR REVIEW

Question 1. What **themes** does Whitman develop?

Answer: *Leaves of Grass* is poetry that celebrates all the dimensions of "self," America, love, life, death, the material and the spiritual. For all these, Whitman becomes the poetic spokesman.

He asserts constantly what he believes to be a pattern of life, death, and rebirth in the universe. Death holds no terror for him, because he believes that it leads only to rebirth as part of an unending cycle.

Whitman denies evil in the traditional sense. He asserts the equality of all things, of all people, and of the body with the soul. He announces his faith in a wholesome and desirable natural freedom in all sexual activity. His celebration of the body accentuates sensual pleasure but discovers social benefit in it as well. Homosexual love ("cohesiveness") is as proper and as unobjectionable in his opinion as male and female love ("amativeness"). For Whitman, male love contains the potential for strong and enduring friendships, those manly bonds of comradeship that appealed to him. In the physical love of man and woman, he sees a creative union producing super generations of the future.

Whitman glorifies the common man. He sees him as a noble part of humanity; and he finds no one, regardless of occupation or condition, unworthy of being saluted in his poetry.

He believes that the real "self" is the "eidolon," the spiritual image or soul behind the outward appearance of things. This image or soul is then part of a great or universal soul.

As the body is as precious as the spirit, so Whitman finds the material as sacred as the spiritual. Pantheistically, he gives his idea of deity material presence in, and identity with, everything in the world. In his belief in evolution and reincarnation, Whitman discovers both a material and a spiritual immortality.

Finding his God in all matter of which he himself is an immortal part, the poet can assert a feeling of fraternal equality with his deity. His God is, therefore, the "great Camerado" whose spirit is the "brother" of his own, a God not "greater to one than one's self is."

Whitman encourages independence and self-reliance, and asserts that love is a strengthening and essential force in the universe. His world is one of eternal optimism and confidence in the evolutionary improvement of all things. He is conscious of his links with the past and the future; but he is aware of his own individuality in the "float," the evolutionary storehouse and flow of nature.

Question 2. Are symbols important in Whitman's poetry?

Answer: Symbols are very important in Whitman's poetry and are bound together with his themes. Outstanding symbols, such as the thrush, mockingbird, lilac, calamus reed, sea, star, and grass all represent important ideas in the individual poems and groups in which they occur.

The mockingbird in "Out of the Cradle Endlessly Rocking" inspires the youthful poet to an awareness of love. However, on mature reflection, Whitman realizes that this was only part of a complete understanding of life and death. The whispering of the word "death" by the sea brought an understanding of a cyclic pattern of death and rebirth and, thereby, brought the poet to poetic maturity.

The lilac with its blossoms symbolized love and rebirth in "When Lilacs Last in the Dooryard Bloom'd." The thrush's call was a summons to a reconciliation and understanding of death by the poet. The star was a symbol of the dead Abraham Lincoln and came to represent the poet's grief for the President. These symbols extend beyond the poet's personal lamentation in their significance; the lilac and thrush represent, on a universal level, Whitman's notions of love, rebirth, and the hopeful acceptance of death.

Whitman stated that the calamus reed represented "the biggest & hardiest kind of spears of grass -and their fresh, aquatic, pungent bouquet." This grass, growing in secluded watery spots, represented male love for the poet; by identifying a "biggest & hardiest" character in it, he colors the aspect of those relationships with a robust quality. The symbol is powerfully sensual; but by its very nature as a type of grass, it is related to Whitman's broad use of the grass symbol discussed in the following question.

Question 3. What does the symbol of the grass represent?

Answer: The symbol of the grass stands above all the other Whitman symbols and draws together the entire span of the poet's ideas. Whitman's infinite cycle of reincarnation is symbolized by the grass in its yearly renewal and growth in a potentially boundless density and area. He intends it to represent his "same old law," not only symbolically, but actually in its continuing organic turnover of matter into new forms. Therefore the grass is symbolic of, as well as part of, the process that it represents. Perhaps the most common of growths, the grass has unity in a wide expanse of single blades. Symbolically, it suggests notions of equality; the common man, individually and collectively; and the broad spirit of democracy itself.

Whitman's grass is significant as far as his poetic form is concerned. As the grass grows naturally and freely, so Whitman's poetry grows in an "organic" fashion. The verse is intended to grow freely out of the needs and nature of the poetry, and not to be contained within an imposed structure. Whitman is extremely successful as a symbolist, and those symbols are the strongest building blocks of his poetry.

Question 4. Did the Civil War affect Whitman's poetry?

Answer: The Civil War had a profound effect on Whitman's poetry. It provided the poetic subjects and the emotional spur that Whitman needed to make a good poet a superior one. It opened fresh directions for him. His faith in American democracy, his intense humanitarianism, and his "manly" affections discovered entirely new avenues of expression. The war and the Union victory justified his faith in the democratic system. The suffering endured by soldiers and civilians drew out the poet's warmest human emotions. The manly love of the *Calamus* poems, once private and personal for him, achieved an open and acceptable expression in the brotherly and fatherly affection prompted by his hospital visits. Whitman poured out his great pictorial powers in *Drum-Taps* and was himself convinced that the Civil War played a major role in the development of *Leaves of Grass*. It is certain that the war carried the poet to the enormously productive and mature period of his poetry in which he created his two great masterpieces, "Out of the Cradle Endlessly Rocking" and "When Lilacs Last in the Dooryard Bloom'd."

Question 5. What are the style, quality, and influence of Whitman's poetry?

Answer: Whitman's basic importance to American literature was early recognized by such important literary and philosophical figures as Ralph Waldo Emerson and Henry David Thoreau. As a poetical innovator, Whitman broke sharply with conventional forms and subjects. The scattered effect of *Leaves of Grass* left the reader accustomed to ordered literary patterns completely at a loss to know what to make of it. Without the usual meters, rhymes, and appearance that sounded and looked like poetry on the printed page, *Leaves of Grass* baffled the public.

Whitman's poetry was sixty to seventy years ahead of its time both in form and in the treatment of themes. The average mid-nineteenth century American who encountered the collection of verse, while not comprehending the poet's purpose, was quick to claim that it violated all the accepted laws of decency as well as of poetry. Literature is often more wisely and objectively evaluated from the perspective of time. This is certainly true of *Leaves of Grass*, for scholarly study can best illuminate both the favorable and the unfavorable characteristics of a literary work when the consideration of that work is not prejudiced by the social standards and literary tastes of the poet's own day.

Today we realize that Walt Whitman is a great American poet. This does not mean that all the poetry that he wrote is undeniably great or that it never offends good taste. Emerson himself objected to the *Children of Adam* poems; and certain passages in *Leaves of Grass*, even when read today, are distasteful to readers.

Critics would agree that various poems and sections of Whitman's poems are basically weak and bear little resemblance to good verse. The merit of Whitman's catalogues has been challenged (see Summary of chapter on "Song of Myself.") A general disunity in the poetry has been cited, along with the unbounded freedom with language, the contrived word orders, an eccentric way of collecting and combining foreign and classical words, and the invention of new words.

If, at his worst, Whitman is unpoetic, at his best he is superb and masterful. His pace impels the reader along, and his **imagery** is sharp and extraordinarily visual. His pictorial powers are keenly observant, whether soaring in a panorama over everyday people and occupations, or paused and fascinated by some striking sight or sound in nature. In his mature poetry, such as "Out of the Cradle" and "When Lilacs Last," he is at the height of his artistic powers in the development of symbols and themes. Whitman's language, if contrived and forced at times, is nevertheless exciting; it is a natural match for the fresh and unorthodox character of his ideas. His poetry has a musical quality of its own; more than that of any other American poet, Whitman's verse has been set to music. Portions of it are not unlike the Italian operas of which he was so fond. The lines of his poetry are often long and rolling in a broad oratorical style and are blended with a strong Biblical tone in some passages.

While his unconventional poetic form on the printed page can present difficulty for the reader, Whitman's poetry is relieved of many of its obstacles when read aloud. If his style and language seem roughly experimental and some of his startling effects appear contrived, it may be part of the price the poet has paid for originality. His persona, overly dramatic and boastful as well as consciously and unconsciously humorous, remains as a good literary device for encircling his wide development of ideas.

Whitman was greatly influenced by Emerson, from whom he surely derived much of his philosophy regarding nature, deity, and a great world-soul in the universe. It was Emerson of whom Whitman said, "I was simmering, simmering, simmering; Emerson brought me to a boil." However much the poet was indebted to others, his remarkable originality cannot be denied. It is difficult to measure precisely Whitman's influence upon later poets. In such modern figures as Hart Crane and Carl Sandburg, the influence is obvious; in many others of the twentieth century, the effect is less plainly evident but strongly felt. However, it is less in his visionary philosophy, and more in a wide-ranging **free verse** form and unrestrained approach to language and **theme**, that he sets a precedent for twentieth century experimentation in poetry.

The stream-of-consciousness technique is a literary device that allows a rambling sequence of ideas and impressions to flow freely through a character's mind. As a major literary technique, it is usually associated with the twentieth century Irish writer James Joyce. In Whitman's great tumble and mixture of private sensation and external universal experience (particularly in "Song of Myself"), something of this same quality is evident.

Sharply contrasting to the Victorian stiffness of his day, the liberal attitudes in *Leaves of Grass* seem the forerunners of many of the social attitudes of the present. His beliefs in equality, his optimistic faith in democracy, his frank approach to subjects that were not openly discussed, and his elevation of the position of women find plentiful examples in our own times.

The complexity of Walt Whitman's poetry is a grand challenge to definition and summary, perhaps an impossible one to answer with finality. The critic Lewis Mumford seems to have been well aware of Whitman's depth and scope when he remarked in 1926, "He is more than a single writer: he is almost a literature."

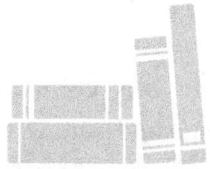

TOPICS FOR RESEARCH REPORTS

....

1. Whitman as the poet of democracy and the common man.

2. Whitman and the critics: the critics in his own day; the critics today. A comparison of British and American reaction to *Leaves of Grass*.

3. **Realism** in *Drum-Taps*.

4. Examples of autobiography in *Leaves of Grass*.

5. Whitman as a pictorial poet.

6. Examples of Whitman's optimism in *Leaves of Grass*.

7. Whitman's use of birds in his poetry.

8. Whitman as a nature poet.

9. The use of sea **imagery** in Whitman's poetry.

10. Walt Whitman and Abraham Lincoln.

11. A comparison between Whitman and a modern poet: for example, Whitman and Carl Sandburg.

12. Symbols: Whitman's use of them and their importance in any single poem or group of poems.

13. A close analysis of any single Whitman poem: vocabulary, themes, **imagery**, mood, form, your personal appreciation, short summary of major critical opinions.

14. Whitman's catalogues: beautiful or clumsy?

15. Whitman's catalogues as expressions of his democratic spirit.

16. The Whitman persona: boastful and confident? - overly dramatic? - comical? - purpose? -what does it accomplish? - is it a successful device?

17. Examples of Whitman's humanitarianism in *Leaves of Grass*.

18. Whitman's curious vocabulary: the coined words, slang, colloquialisms, foreign words. (In any poem or group of poems.)

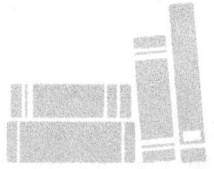

ANNOTATED BIBLIOGRAPHICAL GUIDE

STANDARD EDITION

The Complete Writings of Walt Whitman, edited by Richard M. Bucke, Thomas B. Harned, and Horace L. Traubel. New York: G. P. Putnam's Sons, 1902 (The Camden Edition). This is still the standard edition of Whitman's work, but it is rapidly becoming obsolete with the gradual appearance of the following:

The Collected Writings of Walt Whitman. New York: New York University Press, 1961. This represents the magnificent new definitive edition under the general editorship of two eminent Whitman scholars, Gay Wilson Allen and Sculley Bradley. To date, several volumes of prose works, correspondence, and early poetry and fiction have appeared. The selections from Whitman's letters that appear in this study guide have been drawn from this edition.

OTHER USEFUL EDITIONS

Walt Whitman: Complete Poetry and Selected Prose, edited by James E. Miller. New York: Riverside Edition of Houghton Mifflin Co., Boston, 1959.

The Portable Whitman, edited by Mark Van Doren. New York: The Viking Press, 1945.

(The above two editions contain fine introductions of considerable value for the student.)

Leaves of Grass and Selected Prose. New York: The Modern Library edition of Random House.

Leaves of Grass. New York: Dolphin Books, Doubleday and Co. This is a faithful paperback reprint of the 1855 first edition which prompted Emerson's letter of praise. There is no introduction included.

SINGLE WHITMAN STUDIES AND COLLECTIONS OF ESSAYS

Allen, Gay Wilson. *Walt Whitman Handbook*. Chicago: Packard and Co., 1946. This volume is an extremely valuable tool for any Whitman student. It contains a survey of Whitman biography to 1946, considers the growth of Leaves through the various editions, examines Whitman's basic ideas, "literary techniques," and "social thought," and places the poet's work in the perspective of "world literature." This is an essential book for a sound understanding of many of Whitman's puzzling aspects.

Allen, Gay Wilson, and Charles T. Davis, editors. *Walt Whitman's Poems: Selections With Critical Aids*. New York: New York University Press, 1955. Some background and a "critical note" are provided for each poem; and the fifty-one page critical introduction is excellent. The book has also been published in an Evergreen paperback edition by Grove Press.

Broderick, John C., editor. *Whitman the Poet: Materials for Study.* California: Wadsworth Publishing Co., 1962. The book contains a group of Whitman prefaces and poems; some of Whitman's "miscellaneous criticisms of books and authors, written mainly for newspapers"; chapters containing essays on the poet's technique, form, style, language, and persona; some early critical estimates of the poet; and a chapter containing six essays on Whitman's poem, "Passage to India." Included is a thorough fifteen-page bibliography of books and articles broken down into several categories.

Lewis, R. W. B., editor. *The Presence of Walt Whitman: Selected Papers from the English Institute* (English Institute Essays). New York: Columbia University Press, 1962. Included in the collection are essays on "Out of the Cradle" as well as comparative studies of Whitman.

Marx, Leo, editor. *The Americanness of Walt Whitman (Problems in American Civilization series).* Boston: D. C. Heath and Co., 1960. This book contains the Harvard philosopher George Santayana's famous 1900 essay attacking Whitman, an essay which still prompts spirited replies from Whitman's critical defenders. The editor has supplied a short introduction and a useful bibliography.

Pearce, Roy Harvey, editor. *Whitman: A Collection of Critical Essays.* (Twentieth Century Views series). New Jersey: Prentice-Hall, Inc., 1962. A broad range of fifteen essays including Whitman evaluations by such twentieth century poets as Ezra Pound, D. H. Lawrence, and William Carlos Williams. The editor has provided a good bibliography that lists periodical articles as well as books.

WHITMAN BIOGRAPHY

Allen, Gay Wilson. *The Solitary Singer: A Critical Biography of Walt Whitman*. New York: The Macmillan Co., 1955. This book remains the definitive Whitman biographical work.

FOREIGN ESTIMATES OF WHITMAN

Allen, Gay Wilson, editor. *Walt Whitman Abroad*. Syracuse: Syracuse University Press, 1955. These are translations of a cross section of foreign scholarship on Whitman.

Asselineau, Roger. *The Evolution of Walt Whitman*. Cambridge, Massachusetts: Harvard University Press (Belknap Press), 1960 and 1962. With the assistance of Richard P. Adams, this is the two-volume English translation of Asselineau's huge work on Whitman originally published in French in 1954. Volume I, *The Creation of a Personality*, 1960, is mainly biographical. Volume II, *The Creation of a Book*, 1962, is a critical effort which examines "the evolution of the great **themes** of *Leaves of Grass* and the development of Whitman's art."

SOURCES FOR THE LATEST WHITMAN SCHOLARSHIP

For current listings of the ever-increasing additions to Whitman scholarship, consult the following publications which are readily available in larger libraries:

The PMLA Annual Bibliography. This publication of The Modern Language Association appears in May of each year.

Walt Whitman Review. This periodical is published quarterly by the Wayne State University Press, Detroit, Michigan.

American Literature. This quarterly periodical is published by the Duke University Press, Durham, North Carolina.

www.ingramcontent.com/pod-product-compliance
Lightning Source LLC
LaVergne TN
LVHW021713060526
838200LV00050B/2638